Balikwas

Balikwas

How to Emigrate to The Philippines

Chris Payne

First published by Authorhouse Inc 2013
Second revised paperback edition published by
Lipa Publishing 2013

© 2013-15 Chris Payne. All rights reserved.

ISBN 978-971-95780-0-0(Paperback)

No part of this book may be reproduced, stored in a retrieval system
or transmitted by any means without the written permission of the author.

Because of the dynamic nature of the Internet, any web addresses
or links contained in this book may have changed since publication
and may no longer be valid.

The views expressed in this book are entirely those of the author.

Lipa Publishing
Helen Street,
Base View Homes
Lipa City, Batangas
The Philippines 4217

Website : http://lipapublishing.com
Email : lipapub@yahoo.com.ph

To Cosette with thanks for all her help

Contents

Foreword	....	1
One	....	7
Two	....	17
Three	....	27
Four	....	35
Five	....	47
Six	....	57
Seven	....	67
Eight	....	73
Nine	....	87
Postscript	....	99
Appendix A - what it all cost us.	....	111
Appendix B - what it costs to live in The Philippines	....	113
Appendix C - what you need to do in your home country before you emigrate.	....	119
Appendix D - what are the customs requirements for The Philippines?	....	125
Appendix E - immigration rules in The Philippines	....	127
Appendix F - addresses	....	131
Acknowledgements	....	133

Balikwas – How to Emigrate to The Philippines

balikwas, magbalikwas, balikwasin

Active Verb: magbalikwas

Passive Verb: balikwasin

English Definition

1) to turn suddenly to the opposite side; to rise suddenly from a lying position (verb)
2) to turn something suddenly to the opposite side (verb)

Example Bumalikwas ako sa kama nang narinig ko ang putok ng baril. (I jumped out of bed when I heard the gunshot.)

Source: *http://www.seasite.niu.edu/Tagalog/*

Balikwas – How to Emigrate to The Philippines

Foreword

Balikwas' is Tagalog, the language of my new country, The Philippines. Like so many Tagalog words, it expresses a subtle idea which is almost untranslatable into English, the language for down-to-earth practicality. The dictionary meaning of balikwas is 'to wake up startled' or 'to turn over to the other side' but it can also stand for the English idea of going against the flow. By deciding to emigrate at an age when many other Englishmen are settling back into relaxed retirement, I am bucking the trend and going against the flow. And, by choosing The Philippines as my new domicile instead of a care home in Bournemouth, I am definitely turning over to the other side, in my case, to the other side of the world.

'Balikwas', with its multiple shades of meaning, also reflects the spirit of my emigration move by its inexactness.. The very imprecision of the Tagalog word mirrors closely my ambiguous feelings for bravely, or foolishly, making a young man's move at an age when most of my English contemporaries are, metaphorically speaking, already tucked up in bed with their Horlicks.

The twenty-first century émigré has it much easier than foreign travellers of previous generations. Wherever he goes in the world, he can look forward to familiar sights and sounds. Skyscraper cityscapes, similar cars and traffic jams, the new universal casual dress code, extensive shopping malls, even that un-nuanced version of English, the *lingua americana*, will all be there to greet him wherever in the world he touches down. Foreign travel is now a very long way from the eye-opening experiences of previous generations of expatriates.

Because of this convergence of international urban cultures to something approximating to that of a city in middle America, it is now very much easier to move abroad because there is little culture shock when one gets there. Many things will be instantly familiar – the shops, for example, will be immediately recognisable – Starbucks, McDonalds, Kentucky Fried Chicken, Marks and Spencer and the up-market designer names are, like God, everywhere. And should you be kicking your heels in the Holiday Inn you will spend a lot of time switching TV channels between Bloomberg, CNN and BBC World. When you get to 'abroad' you will find much else besides the retailers that are familiar. The rules of courtesy and good manners apply universally, the bureaucrats are identical jobsworths whether you are in Todmorden or Tokyo. The immigration procedures are always labyrinthine, confusing and (deliberately?) intimidating. And I have yet to visit a foreign city where I did not, at some time during my stay, attract, by my English accent, the attentions of some young man who would start a conversation with me on the subject of that outstanding global brand, Manchester United.

Emigration is made easier these days because of two major scientific advances. The first is the ubiquitous computer. Modern information technology, including social networks, Skype™ and emails shrinks the distance between self and loved ones across the oceans. Most people now have access to computer technology unimaginable only a few decades ago. The modern laptop or desktop or hand-held machine has the sort of computing power which an entire developed country might have laid claim to as recently as the 1960's, a long-ago era when letters were still the usual long-distance communication medium, because telephones were so unreliable and expensive. In 1960, a letter might take a week to cross the globe via air mail, or six weeks if sent on a ship.

The other factor affecting one's attitude to emigration is the availability of cheap air travel. Until the 1980's air travel was prohibitively expensive. Using an aeroplane was the privilege of the rich and glamorous. For example, the scheduled air fare from London to Milan in 1980 was about £400 and the cost of a long haul flight to the Far East might run into thousands of pounds. But since then, competition between airlines and the design of more efficient aircraft have brought fares down to what an ordinary person can afford. Mass air travel is no longer smart and exciting, quite the opposite, but it has democratised international tourism. Resultingly, it has also broadened the minds and extended the life choices of very many people.

So, even in The Philippines, I don't feel any impression of having travelled so very far. I have no sense, as a Victorian traveller might have had, that I had fallen off the edge of the world. I am only ever microseconds away from face-to-face communication with my friends and family in Europe. And, should an urgent return be necessary then I am only twenty hours, or thereabouts, from London by plane.

Emigration is, now, no longer the sort of once-in-a-lifetime, no-turning-back deal it was until a generation ago. It is a lifestyle choice made, these days, not just by the young and footloose. Increasingly older people, and not just the jet-setting rich, are seeing the benefits of living in other countries. It is reported on the UK Office of National Statistics website, for example, that net emigration from the UK for other than work-related reasons is currently running at about 150,000 per year. Many of this number will be retirees to warmer, more affordable, countries. I was told by the UK Department of Works and Pensions, when I phoned them in 2011 about pension entitlements for Britons resident abroad, that there are about five thousand retired Britons currently receiving their state pensions through Philippine banks. Nor is it any surprise that one of the most successful British films of 2011, was *The Best Exotic Marigold Hotel* starring some of the cream of British acting talent. This film, which tracks the adventures of a group of British pensioners setting off for retirement in India, resonated strongly. The very idea of retirement to the tropics away from cold, wet England, is clearly in the air.

The UK, one realises, once one has spent some time abroad, can be quite a stressful place to live, and a major cause of the stress is the famous English weather. You have to be tough to be old, as the saying goes. For many older British, the winter cold can be an annual torture. I, a graduate of dozens of English winters, lost my sense of winter wonderland enchantment sometime in the 1950's. Now, at seventy, the English winter is, for me, nothing more than a bad time of the year which one must endure and get through as best as possible. Its charm soon wears off. My Filipina wife, Loydz, spent, in 2010, her first English winter in the north of England. At first she was enchanted by the snow – the first she had ever seen. She spent time in the garden and out on the street, taking numerous photographs for her Facebook wall to show off to her friends back home. By her second winter, the spell had been completely broken - she 'went native' as we spent most of the time in the house with the heating turned up.

A side effect of the new world of instant communication has been the rise of the number of relationships between people who, in previous generations, would never have met. Or, if they had met in colonial times, there would have been too great a social gulf to permit of any relationship based on mutual respect and social equality. But cheap air travel and information technology have opened up the world to all sorts of interesting new partnerships. In my childhood, one chose one's life partner from a narrow set of potential consorts drawn exclusively from one's social class and the local neighbourhood. By contrast, I met my dear wife Loydz on an Internet dating site. In previous eras, our meeting would have been well-nigh impossible.

We have lived in several countries in our short marriage. She spent some time with me in Europe and fully adjusted to life there. Now it is my turn, my formal academic career being over and my being well into retirement, to move to my wife's home country and make a new life amid her warm, friendly, industrious compatriots. This returning of the compliment also has a Tagalog word, 'balikwasan' derived, etymologically, from 'balikwas'.

Overall, the time line of what we came to regard as the 'project' consumed approximately a biologically appropriate nine months from the late summer of 2012 until the spring of 2013. Any doubts that we might be doing the wrong thing were dispelled by a separation enforced on us by the United Kingdom Border Agency who would not allow Loydz a visa to return to the UK. Because she was stranded in Manila while I was back in England, we were able to separate the project into two parts working in parallel. Loydz became project manager of the Philippine end of the operation, and supervised the building of our new house there. I took over the sale of the British house, the packing and financing. Our efforts dovetailed nicely. As it turned out, there was only a few weeks' hiatus between the completions of the selling up and the building.

This book is an account of how we made the change from the UK to The Philippines. It is written as a memoir because that is a more interesting format than a mere how-to-do-it textbook. I have left out a lot of descriptive detail about my new country because I am not writing a travelogue. Hopefully, my book will also be of use to intrepid emigrants to other countries than the Philippines since the overall experience is basically the same whatever country one is moving to. I hope our experiences can be made use of by others. Hopefully, if I have got the format right, this report may be equally readable as a story of how a pensioner and his wife set up home in a far-off country, while being also an instruction manual of what one needs to do should one be contemplating doing the same thing oneself.

Balikwas – How to Emigrate to The Philippines

One

They, the counsellors and the 'people people', do say that in the hierarchy of stressful experiences, moving house comes in the top three, right after death and divorce. Emigration is house-moving taken to extremes. It involves a million small details, administrative, financial and social, which need to be co-ordinated, scheduled and implemented. For the reasons why we chose to embark on this particular journey, a little background is first required.

Loydz and I married in 2006 and spent the first five years of our married life in a number of foreign countries – Germany, France, Cyprus and Bulgaria - with only short visits to our home countries of the The Philippines and the UK This itinerant lifestyle was forced on us by the demands of my job as a untenured university professor of IT working a sequence of short contracts as and where they came up. I was already too old for permanent academic employment, which, in the UK, means being under 65. But I was in regular demand from those American universities abroad who do not practise institutional ageism.

We had had a nice house in Brittany where we had spent most of 2007. But Loydz was unhappy there and, during my time in Cyprus, (2007-2009) at Girne American University in Kyrenia, we started to think about selling up in France and moving to England, my home country, for permanent retirement. After the Cyprus contract came to an end and I had been head-hunted by the American University in Bulgaria or AUBG, we moved, in early 2009, to the provincial Bulgarian city of Blagoevgrad. It was shortly after we arrived there that news came through that we had a buyer for our Breton *longère*.

It was while we were in Bulgaria that we started to make our long-term plans. Where, in the UK, would we make our permanent retirement? We made a shortlist of possible towns. Having neither jobs nor children at school, there were no constraints on our final choice, save that it be affordable to a couple who would be living on pension income only. We settled on Lincoln, a fine historic city where we bought a small house into which we moved in May 2009. In the autumn of that year and throughout 2011, I worked some short contracts at AUBG in between which we made a comfortable home for ourselves in Lincoln.

So, what was it, after all these peregrinations that prompted us to up sticks and emigrate to The Philippines? Life in England was pleasant enough and we soon got into the easy routine of millions of older British couples – trips out to antiques fairs, car boot sales and galleries, a weekly shop at Tesco, Loydz' Sunday mass at the local Catholic church, cooking, TV, pottering about in the shed, the occasional trip to London, shopping, a weekly meal out and so on. It was very simple and easy.

So why change? What is the downside of this relaxed way of life? Well, there were three main problems. In a word each, they are money, climate and bureaucracy.

First, money. I had an adequate pension for the simple life I have just described. But adequate was all it was – the budget was very tight. The cost of living in the UK is somewhere near the very highest in the world. So much so that the country is routinely referred to as 'Treasure Island' by some foreign companies because they can charge the British much higher prices than elsewhere. Living in England, one is constantly amazed at how expensive everything is. For example, a ten minute checkup at the dentist will cost a hundred dollars, a one-mile taxi ride is ten dollars. Parking on a piece of waste land in the centre of Lincoln costs $5 an hour. And I never once got to understand whatever I got in return for the hundred pounds a month I paid to the local council for its 'services'. A ticket to watch first class football in the English Premier League will cost up to £62, or about $100. Even to watch, say, Bayern Munich, one will pay no more than 20 Euros and Germany is not a cheap country either. A common remark, which my American friends invariably make when they visit me in England is 'just where does all that money go?'

As well as the high cost of everything, there was continuous inflation. The British government was keen to tell us that inflation was containable at about 4%. Our experience was that prices were going up much faster than that, at about 10% a year. All this made us fearful that we might slip into that class of UK pensioner who have, every winter, to make a desperate choice between buying food and heating their homes.

I suppose that with a modest pension from my thirty years as a teacher in England and the small statutory state pension, I could provide at a basic level for myself and my wife. We were probably a bit better off than others of my age even if our income did not extend to anything more than modest comfort. We were also living in a house not dissimilar to the one I had grown up in. In fact it had an identical layout to the 3-bed semi-detached council house where I spent some of my formative years, but now privatised and upgraded with extras like central heating. I sometimes considered how short was the social and financial distance I had travelled in the nearly sixty years of continuous employment between my first paper round and my final retirement as a university professor.

The English climate, especially in winter, is not particularly clement. In fact, it is, to put it simply, downright miserable. We spent the whole of 2010 at home in Lincoln. The weather was, for about 80% of the time, the same – mild, windy and overcast with grey cloud. There were variations from this norm in the other twenty per cent of the year. There was a brief heat wave in June and heavy snowfalls at each end of the year. For many Englishmen, and I used to be one of them, such weather patterns are what one is used to and one knows how to cope with them. Cold? Then put another sweater on! One adapts to one's environment and doesn't think about it. But having travelled widely, I now missed the sunshine of continental, and especially Mediterranean, Europe, where I had spent much of the previous two decades. And, for Loydz, once the novelties of buying warm clothes and the first sight of snow had worn off, the cold weather was often near unbearable.

Many of my countrymen enjoy this predictability and the opportunities it gives for human contact. When a day is slightly less cold or slightly more sunny than yesterday, 'not bad for the time of year,' one might say to the neighbour one has avoided for most of the year. 'Looks like rain,' he will reply in time-honoured fashion. A rare hot sunny day or the two or three days of snow in January will still be celebrated in press and on TV as almost supra-normal events. Much to the amusement of the citizens of most other northern countries where it is normal practice to anticipate that winter will bring winter weather, half an inch of snow in January – 'What? Snow in January!! Heaven forfend!' - will still close the British airports and train services, shut the schools and bring gloomy forecasts of impending apocalyptic economic collapse.

But the third, the most serious reason which forced our hand, was our treatment at the hands of the United Kingdom Border Agency, the UKBA, a quasi-autonomous governmental organisation, or QUANGO, which has overall responsibility for policing Britain's borders and issuing visas for entry to the Promised Land. For several years, from the very start of our marriage, we had been involved in what had seemed like a continuous running war of attrition with them.

Don't get me wrong about the UKBA. I can quite see that such a border guardian is essential in today's world of mass travel. The UKBA does an important job in keeping the UK closed to the sort of malevolent evil-doers who bring terror to British streets. Nor do I have any problem with their activities when it comes to keeping out economic migrants who have no more connection with the UK than a certificate in English as a Foreign Language from some junk college in a far-off city. I am happy that the UKBA erects its barriers against those whose only purpose in coming to the UK is to take unfair advantage of Britain's generous social security and health services. In order to guard the borders effectively against all these undesirables, the UKBA has created a huge bureaucracy of box-tickers and nay-sayers whose default position is to make UK entry as difficult as possible and to turn down automatically any application for entry which has a single unticked box.

Over the years, we had made, on Loydz', behalf, numerous applications to obtain a long-stay visa for her to remain in the UK for extended periods of time. Having been turned down repeatedly on this pretext or that, we had, over the three years when we lived in Lincoln, come to realise that her getting into the UK as a permanent resident would be a near-impossibility. It was after a particularly lunatic *diktat* that we started to change our minds about making our permanent home in the UK.

Because of our itinerant life-style, Loydz always had to rely for entry to the UK on short-stay, two-year visas. In the summer of 2010, her latest short stay visa was coming up to its expiration. We drove from Lincoln to Sheffield, where the UKBA has an office, and tried to make an application there for a renewal of it. No, the counter clerk told us, you cannot do that here, you must re-apply in Manila. So we packed up the large file of documents – one accumulates myriads of data in this unrelenting struggle – and put her on a plane for Manila. She then deposited this file with a company called VFS Inc., to which the UKBA outsources its visa processing in The Philippines. This same VFS then sent this huge file back to the UK for the decision which was, in turn, relayed back to Manila, so that she could return to England for another two years. Total costs including fees and fares etc for all this futility – about £2000. It was then that we realised the enormousness of the task of getting British residency for a Filipina, even one married to an Englishman and being co-owner of an English house. She had also passed, first time, the *Living in the UK* citizenship test. She is, of course, perfectly fluent in English and a university graduate - which just about makes her the sort of dangerous subversive which the UKBA was set up to exclude.

As a result of these experiences with the UKBA we were starting to get more serious about finding a permanent home outside the UK. But we decided to give it one last shot. Her two-year short-stay spouse visa was coming up for renewal in September 2012 and we had read on the UKBA website that we could apply for her naturalisation after we had been domiciled in the UK for three years, which we had been, since it was now over three years since we had first bought our house in Lincoln. We downloaded the form and sent it off by DHL courier, together with the usual sheaf of supporting documentation and the fee - £845, non-refundable. All UKBA's extortionate fees, the highest immigration fees in the world, are, of course, non-refundable even if, as I suspect is their usual practice, all they do in exchange for the money is to cash the cheque and send out an automatic refusal.

Shortly after this, we received news that Loydz' mother had been taken seriously ill in Manila. Loydz, as the *ate,* or senior daughter, was obliged to go back to care for her. This meant we had to ask the UKBA to return her passport. We phoned the UKBA office in Liverpool and, after half an hour or so, reached someone who would speak to us. The first thing the woman told us was that our application for naturalisation had been premature and that before one could apply for naturalisation, we would need first to make a separate application for Indefinite Leave to Remain. The need to secure this intermediate award before going for full naturalisation is not something which is explained on the UKBA website. The UKBA had taken our money and accepted out application so we assumed we had followed the rules as they had laid them down. The woman at the UKBA then told us that she would return the passport in ten days but that Loydz' application would then go to the bottom of the pack. Actually, it didn't arrive in ten days, so in order to get her flight to Manila, Loydz needed to get a special once-only travel document from the Philippine Embassy in London. The passport was eventually sent back to Lincoln and the expected refusal of naturalisation appeared shortly after that.

But that was not quite the end. Without naturalisation and with an expired short-stay visa, Loydz now made a new expensive visa application to VFS in Manila for another short-stay spouse visa like the ones she had had twice before. This was refused on the grounds that since she had been turned down for naturalisation, she was therefore no longer eligible for any lesser visa because that would be merely a ploy by her to get into England 'by the back door'. Once in the UK, she was told, she would stay on as an illegal immigrant. We made several appeals against this arbitrariness but each was answered by a bland form letter from a different Filipino officer. So Loydz was stuck in Manila and I was still in Lincoln. The only way we could continue our married life would be for me to sell up the Lincoln house as quickly as possible and move to The Philippines.

These struggles against the UKBA had tired us out emotionally. The British government had finally defeated us. They had won. We were beaten. We had lost the stomach for the fight. I can only congratulate them on their crushing victory over a seventy-year-old pensioner and his harmless Filipina wife. Looked at one way, though, their victory could be thought of as oddly reassuring. Just think, if they will put so such energy into keeping Britain free of a middle-aged housewife who has a house in the UK and a respectable British husband, then think how much more effort will they be putting in when it comes to keeping out those really bad people they are always warning us about.

Since we had been anticipating immigration problems ever since the lunacy of incident with the Sheffield UKBA office we were mentally preparing ourselves for a move to somewhere else. At first we considered Spain. We spoke to a Spanish lawyer at the 'Home in the Sun' exhibition at Olympia. He told us that Filipinos are preferentially welcome in Spain by virtue of residual Spanish colonial guilt. We started looking at Spanish real estate websites and even bought a language course. We also put the Lincoln house on the market with a well-known chain of estate agents. As the economic news from Spain got worse though, we started to lose our enthusiasm for that country. Stories about shortages of medications and security concerns prompted us to think again.

The choice of estate agent was another mistake. We chose one, a large well-known chain, with an eccentric pricing process. We had bought the house in 2009 for £90,000 and we had probably spent about £5-6000 on improving it. It was small and easy to manage. But the housing market had stalled in the meantime so we looked around at house prices in the neighbourhood and asked the agent to try to sell it for £95,000. In reality this is a loss because in the three years we had lived in the house, there had been not less than 4%, probably more, general inflation every year.

What we will do, the estate agent told us, is set a range of guide price of £95,000 to £105,000. Now this approach may work in a rising, seller's market, but in a static market where buyers are scarce, no-one is going to offer a penny above the bottom price in a range. In this time of austerity, there is little likelihood of what the British call 'gazumping', when the seller accepts an offer but before the contracts are drawn up, which may be weeks later, the buyer is gazumped, or overbid, by someone else who comes in with a higher offer. Unethical, of course, and only in England, where the initial handshake is not worth the paper it is printed on. In Scotland and other countries where I have lived, one's first oral offer, if accepted, becomes a legally binding contract.

In a slow market as now, because housing finance is difficult to come by, the problem we had to live with was the fear of the opposite practice, 'gazundering', where the buyer's first offer prompts the seller to commit to his own move only to find that the buyer reduces his offer price at the last minute.

The estate agent sent a few potential buyers, some of whom made enquiries about a price below the bottom of the range. After a couple of weeks or so with no firm offer, the estate agent got back to us. What we propose, is to widen the price range.

'Yes?' we asked.

'Yes,' the young lady explained to us, as if to mentally deficient children, 'if we widen the range to between £85,000 and £105,000, then we will attract more people. Especially online.'

'But isn't it normal, and experience so far shows that it is, that the lower end of the range is taken as the initial upper negotiating price. The buyers then expect a further discount on that.'

'You don't understand, Mr Payne. A wider range will bring in more people. '

'Well,' I replied, 'I don't intend to sell for much less than £95,000. We are not under pressure for jobs or schools so we will just sit it out.'

'I don't think you will get many visitors unless you widen the range.' A subtle threat.

'Well, then, please send who you can.'

I was right. We got a few offers in the £75,000-£85,000 range and turned them all down. The result was that the estate agents lost interest in trying to force us into giving them a quick commission by our taking a heavy loss. Pretty soon they stopped sending people altogether. Both they and we lost heart in continuing to do business together. One wonders how many people are taken in by such a transparent scam. For an unsophisticated person under unfamiliar pressure and unused to selling a house, the scam is particularly heartless.

We withdrew the house from the market in 2011, when I was offered three new teaching contracts in Bulgaria. When we started to sell it again in early 2012 we were still with the same agents but they sent us no potential buyers, so we waited until we could decide what we were going to do. It soon became obvious to us that The Philippines was the natural option for our future home. It offers all the advantages missing from the UK – the climate is warm, the cost of living is modest and, most importantly, unlike the UK it offers a hospitable welcome to the foreign spouses of its citizens.

In June 2012, we fired, not without a little acrimony, the estate agents who had been so useless and put the house sale with a different agency which appeared to be having a bit more success in selling houses in our area and who did not go in for any silly 'price range guide' nonsense.

* * *

Two

By mid-August 2012, the decision to make our home in The Philippines had been made. Loydz was stuck in Manila, courtesy of our good friends at the UKBA and VFS, with the return half of her air ticket, dated November 1st which was now unusable. But there was one glimmer of good news. The new replacement estate agents were doing their job properly and sending us a steady supply of potential buyers who were serious and prepared to negotiate on price without expecting us to offer to take what the financial world calls a 'haircut'. I would regularly reassure Loydz by email or Skype that a firm buyer's offer would turn up. And sure enough, at the beginning of September, a young couple made an offer. There was a little token haggling for form's sake before a price of £92,000 was agreed. The man seemed to have no financial problems or so he told me, and I had no reason not to believe him. When he confirmed his offer in writing with our new estate agents, it was the signal for Loydz to start looking for somewhere for us to live in The Philippines.

The first question was where? Manila, the capital, is a city which has grown fast. It has a quaint Spanish colonial core around the cathedral, called Intramuros, which has antique shops, galleries, restaurants and so on. But outside that, Manila is a hard-working city with, frankly, not too much charm. Tower blocks, expressways, it has all the hallmarks of a city which has modernised in a hurry. One needs energy to live in a big city. They are for the fast-living, hard-working young. I prefer the ambience of a small town in easy reach of the countryside. I still remember an epiphanic moment some twenty years previously when I had still been in my fifties. I exited from Bond Street tube station in London one day at rush hour to come out into an ocean of young people. I remember thinking at the time that even twenty years before then, I would still have been older than almost everyone I could see. On the other hand, we did not want to live too far from the capital. Loydz has a very large extended family with whom she likes to keep in very close touch. Added to which there would always need to be regular visits to the capital for medical, financial and bureaucratic reasons. After long consideration, we eliminated Subic Bay, a free trade area in northern Luzon which had formerly been a United States Navy deep water port and which still has good cheap left-over ex-USN housing. We also eliminated Baguio, The Philippines' second city, which is at least six hours drive from Manila. From my point of view, Baguio City never sounded very attractive. Every time anyone mentioned it, they would tell me how much I would like it – 'the climate is very European'. My sentiments were not unlike those I had felt when I was looking for somewhere to live in France. 'You will like this village, Monsieur. There are many English living in it,' a lady estate agent told me. 'But, Madame, if I had wanted to live among the English, I could have stayed in London.'

Manila is large enough that it has numerous satellite towns as well as miles and miles of suburbs. We did consider the outer suburbs of Cavite and Tagaytay, where many middle-class Filipinos live and commute into the capital. We dismissed these because house prices in them are inflated as The Philippines seems to be undergoing a permanent housing boom. Seeing we would not be commuting, after Loydz' previous employer in Intramuros had made it clear that she was now too old, at 55, to be re-employed, we therefore decided on Lipa City, Batangas.

Lipa is a smallish city about 70 km from Manila to which it is connected by a fast toll motorway called the South Luzon Expressway, or SLEX. Several competing bus companies provide a regular service between there and the bus station in Makati, the financial district of Metro Manila. Over the month of January 2013, while we were waiting for the house to be completed and living temporarily in a condominium in Manila, we frequently made the trip by bus. Lipa has all the amenities of a modern city including good shops and supermarkets. But overall its scale is more human than Manila's. We would therefore, we decided, become Lipeños and we would make a home there.

The Philippine preference is not to buy second hand houses, unlike the British who suspect the new and consequently prefer something older and more mature with, hopefully, something the British call 'character'.

Filipinos prefer to buy new houses built to order. This is because building materials decay faster in the tropics and houses previously occupied may well come with expensive structural problems. New houses are therefore, for similar reasons, only guaranteed for one year against building defects as compared with a usual ten years for new houses built in the UK.

If one is looking to buy accommodation in The Philippines, one need not go far. In all centres of population one cannot avoid the many touts handing out flyers for condominiums in tower blocks or build-to-order villas in designated domestic building sites called 'subdivisions'. In The Philippines, land for building is cheap and plentiful and financing is readily available in what is an economy on the edge of the Asian boom. A young couple setting out on buying a house will not even need to save up a large initial deposit for their new home. Even this can be financed and paid for in instalments.

Many Filipinos work abroad where they provide cheap labour as drivers, seamen, domestic workers, security guards etc. The Philippine government makes special provision for this large army in its tax codes and money transfer regulations – the foreign currency is very welcome. Such overseas workers are often remitting funds to be invested in the housing market either for their own use or as investments. This is the real driving force of the Philippines housing market. Actually, the workforce of Filipinos abroad is gradually changing its character. From being mainly menial workers, it now includes an increasing number of young professionals - doctors, dentists, nurses and so on. My stepdaughter's husband, for example, is a graduate ship's engineer.

As soon as the decision to move to Lipa had been made, Loydz visited several used houses, thinking that a used house would, if it had not deteriorated so much, have the advantage of being quick to move into. Unlike a new build which would take time, especially since dragging out the time to completion is a universal privilege of the building profession. But the houses she saw were mostly not inside a subdivision. This is important, since subdivisions are usually gated communities with licensed armed guards on the gates and strict inspection of entry permits. Maybe I am being over-cautious here but a European is probably a natural target for muggers or worse. There is still a commonly held local opinion that all foreigners are multi-millionaires. If I am a millionaire then I am a peso millionaire only and certainly not worth mugging. But better to be safe and the security arrangements at the gated community sounded good to me.

At the invitation of Cosette, one of her thirty-seven first cousins (I have mentioned, haven't I, that Loydz has a large extended family?), Loydz visited Base View Homes Subdivision where she met Engineer Vic Maralit, property developer, who was about to become our builder. Vic also introduced her to an architect who provided a full set of architect's drawings which could be modified to the client's taste. After consulting me by email, we agreed to commission a house from Vic in this gated community. Loydz modified the standard design so that the third bedroom was replaced by a tall atrium on the ground floor. Many other details would need to be agreed on as the work progressed.

The mechanism for house buying is principally the same as in the UK with one main difference which is that the purchase of the land (or 'lot', as it is known) is separate from the purchase of the building which is going to stand on it. Lots on Base View Homes are in units of 120 square metres and we needed two of them, numbered 9 and 11. On this 240 square metres would be erected the new modern Chateau Payne.

The cost of the lots was P5000 per square metre, a total of P1.2million (approximately £18,000 or $30,000) less 10% for cash. For a lot of Filipinos, this payment needs to be financed, as I mentioned earlier, and paid for in instalments. We, however, were going to rely on proceeds from the sale of our house in England.

Building would start with the first payment of P1million (about £15,000 or $25,000). The overall cost of building and land would, it was agreed, be paid in four stages. The cost of lot and the first instalment of building costs would be paid on October 1st with a payment of P2.08 million or approximately £33,000. A further million pesos would become due on each of November 1st and December 1st. There would then be a final signing-off payment of P200,000 due on completion, the date of which was contracted for January 23rd 2013. (Full details of what everything cost are given in Appendix A.)

By late September 2012 the buyer for our British house confirmed his intention to proceed with the purchase. He had already engaged a lawyer (called a 'solicitor' in England) for the transaction and he was, we were assured by our estate agents in Lincoln, earnestly looking for a 45% mortgage for the purchase and which he had every confidence of securing. Mortgage finance has been difficult to obtain in the UK since the banking crisis of 2008 but our buyer was only seeking a relatively small mortgage, so we were as confident as we could be that he would go through with the deal and not try to gazunder us.

The next step was to raise, and raise quickly, the £33,000 needed to buy the lot and get the building started. When I had been involved in buying houses much earlier in my life, I had occasionally to use what was called 'bridging' finance while awaiting the funds from the sale to come through. In those days one could raise a proportion of the house equity as a short-term loan until the sale had been completed. I therefore approached Barclays Bank, where I had held an account since 1975. They must have approved of me as a retail client because they had designated me one of their 'Platinum' customers, whatever that means. But they had given me a generous overdraft limit and regularly extended the line of credit on my VISA card.

I spoke to a smart young woman called Chrissie. When I mentioned bridging finance, I got the distinct impression that she was stifling a laugh. 'Bridging finance?' she asked incredulously with a smile, as if I had asked for my account to be converted to pieces of eight or silver doubloons. 'I'm afraid we don't do bridging finance any more. Not for a long time.'

I then outlined my problem to which she offered a part-solution.

'You could borrow a maximum of twenty-five thousand as a personal loan from us or you could go to a private finance company. They might do bridging finance. You could make up the difference on your VISA card. If you time it right, you could not need to pay credit card interest before the house sale is completed.'

I went away to ponder my options. I would need £33,000 immediately and another £15,000 to meet the one million pesos due in November. Using the Internet, I located a number of companies offering private bridging finance. All said pretty much the same thing, that to borrow £30,000 for two or three months would cost about £5,000 in set-up-, legal-, interest- and early redemption charges. One firm told me that it would not cost much more to borrow a million pounds. I decided that there had to be a less-expensive way of doing it.

Fortunately I still did have some savings and I used these to make the first transfer of £33,000 on October 1st. Here I learned a very useful piece of information. One can transfer money from the UK to The Philippines either by converting the pounds to pesos first and sending pesos or by sending pounds and having the receiving bank convert the pounds to pesos in The Philippines. Importantly, the methods use vastly different exchange rates. If I converted the pounds first, I was offered, in September 2012, an exchange rate of 62 pesos to the pound. But the Philippines bank would give me 66 pesos to the pound. This 4 peso per pound difference amounts to P132,000 on my £33,000 transaction, or about two thousand pounds. Indeed, such is the Philippine demand for hard currency, we also found that the street money-changers would often give a better rate than the Philippine banks. The street money changers also prefer large denomination banknotes. Thus, if one is travelling to Manila, it will, almost certainly, be advantageous to take your cash in fifty pound notes rather than to incur the interest charges from using foreign ATM's or, even worse, buying your pesos in the UK first. The very worst deals are to be found at the commercial *bureaux de change* at airports whose rates are ruinous.

Another problem with sending money to The Philippines is that most UK High Street banks charge quite expensive transfer fees. My wife had already opened a joint account for the project at a bank she had once worked at, called The United Coconut Planters Bank or UCPB. My transaction from Barclays to the UCPB had cost me £25, which is not a large premium on the sum I was sending. But it did occur to me that, at some point in the future, I would need to transfer my pension income in much smaller amounts on a regular basis when this overhead would be proportionately more onerous.

There are several solutions to this problem. The first is to take one's account to a bank which has branches in both the UK and in The Philippines, which Barclays does not have. Then one can transfer funds internally between accounts in the two countries. One such bank which provides this service, for its 'Premium' customers at least, is the HSBC, the Hong Kong and Shanghai Banking Corporation, known colloquially as the 'Honkers and Shankers'.

The second solution is to use one of the many private services for money transfer who will do what the banks do but at a lower cost. I have no experience of these but I have heard good reports of their usefulness and their affordability.

Another way one can send money is to use a service like Western Union which has branches everywhere. It works well enough but its charges are commensurate with those of the regular banks. It is useful for sending small emergency funds quickly but one needs access to one of their offices, which may be some distance away.

Finally, one can have one's UK income – pensions etc – paid directly into your foreign account. I understand that the Department of Work and Pensions has recently started to extend this service to Philippine banks. I do not personally favour this. All my income is in the form of pension payments from the UK government, so the transfer route which I eventually chose, which is to have my pensions paid to the HSBC in the UK means that I could make free transfers at will from sterling to pesos. I hope that this method will be less vulnerable to any possible future banking upsets. But I am not sure.

For small-scale funding such as my wife's living costs while she was on her own in Manila, I made transfers to her British Barclays' account and she was able to use her debit card in the Philippine ATM's. This is only a short term solution and it only works for relatively small sums, since most banks are very wary if a card looks as if it is being used wrongly in some way - at which point they will cancel the privilege without notice. Sensible enough, I suppose, but one could easily find oneself financially embarrassed if one's card were rejected without notice at a remote ATM. The exchange rate she got by getting cash this way was acceptable - about P64 to the pound (only slightly below the spot rate of P66 then in force) but there was a charge of P200 pesos for each withdrawal and the daily limit was set at only P14,000 (about £218). After she had become stranded in Manila, she had had to make an expensive international phone call to the Barclays international call centre to extend the time period when she could use her card abroad.

Just about this time, the estate agents put us in touch with lawyers who would handle the conveyancing of the house, as the legal processes of house-selling are called in England. Langleys Solicitors of Lincoln have a large glossy office near the Lincoln Outer Ring Road and I contacted them to try to fix details of the final completion date. The way the British house sale works is that nothing much seems to happen for a long time while the lawyers check the land titles, finances and *bona fide*'s of the two parties. Then two significant dates are set. The first is the date for the exchange of contracts between lawyers when the sale becomes binding on both parties and the buyer must provide 10% of the funds of the sale. The second date is the agreed date for final completion of the sale when the seller receives his payment and must vacate the house at an agreed time on that day, by handing his keys over to the estate agent for collection by the new owner. In my first visit to Langleys I was warned of the vital importance of not handing over the keys until I had actually seen the money in my bank account.

The eccentric British way of selling a house has its roots deep in antiquity. The very title 'estate agent' gives the game away. Originally, estate agents sold landed estates for rich men with vast holdings. Some of them still do, although the average High Street estate agent, as used by the majority of the house buyers and sellers is nowhere near so grand. They are, these days, little more than shops. But the old traditions of estate agency, when every acre of land, every tenant rent and every cow or chicken had to be meticulously accounted for, continue even when the clients are Mr and Mrs Everybody who just want to buy a modest semi-detached starter home on a bog-standard development.

***

Three

The Filipino building contractor, with a degree in engineering, is entitled to call himself 'Engineer', in a society which loves titles. Anyone with a law degree is addressed as 'Attorney' and even the women in the retail optician, if they are graduates, will refer to each other as 'Doctor'. It is a charming, even a touching, feature of a society whose people are famous for their modesty and self-effacement.

Filipinos are also very keen on marking significant events with a ceremony. For example, the new house, when it was eventually be built, would need a blessing from the local priest and no Filipino will drive a new car which has not been, for a few pesos, also blessed so that its occupants will be rendered safe from automobile mishaps. Oddest of all, to an Englishman, is the ceremony of the 'debut', based, I suppose, on the famous Queen Charlotte Ball, when upper class young English women used to be presented to the Queen, as a prelude to a 'season' of dances and parties which were, in actuality, little more than an expensive marriage meat market. This anachronism, and the changing status of women in society saw the English version of the debut terminated in 1958. But it still lives on in The Philippines, when middle class eighteen-year-old women 'come out' as 'debutantes' at a grand party when they attain their majority.

So, before the workers could get going there was the ground-breaking ceremony when three white chickens were sacrificed and their blood sprinkled on the lot to ensure good health and fortune to the occupants of the house. They were subsequently given to the workers for lunch. (It's a very Catholic country.)

Because so many of the workers would be itinerant, they would be living near their work. Before building our house, they had first to construct a large temporary structure for their own living quarters. So,
immediately after the chicken-slaughtering, the first job, to be done quickly because the rainy season was underway, would be to build

themselves a wooden-framed, canvas-covered 'bunk house'. Only then could work really start on our place.

The contract was drawn up with Engineer Vic that the house would be finished by January 23rd 2013. Payments would be staged in November and December with a final P200,000 due after completion. In Lincoln, I negotiated a provisional, tentative, date for completion of the sale of November 30th, with exchange of contracts at or about November 15th. This now gave us a schedule to aim at.

We were blessed by Loydz' familial connections. Her army of cousins was unfailingly helpful to her, and, being generous Filipinos, happily included me in their many kindnesses. It just so happened that one of her favourite cousins, Cosette, also lives in Lipa. Cosette, not having a full-time job herself, gave generously of her time and services as a driver so that Loydz would be able to visit the building site regularly to supervise, as project manager, the progress of the works. We were helped in keeping up the project's momentum by the assistance of Cosette's husband, Bobi, who turned out to be an extremely useful go-between with Engineer Vic. As a senior member of the building department of the Lipa Municipal Authority, one of his duties was the issuing or with-holding of city building permits.

Building projects do not move at a steady rate. There is an initial flurry of activity when walls go up quickly and the roof is put on. At this point, the casual observer would think that the job was nearly finished. This is not the case. A house can look even 80% complete but those final details are where the time will be consumed. Engineer Vic regularly showed us spreadsheets of project plans and building costs and, as far as we could tell, he would indeed meet his various deadlines.

I have moved house several times in my life and I know that there are always a lot of details to follow up even after the sale has been completed. I thought it would make sense to give myself a week or two to tie up various loose ends so that nothing remained when I finally left the UK. I needed also to visit my consultant ophthalmologist, the brilliant Christopher Knapp, at Lincoln Hospital, a visit scheduled for December

13th. I sat down and wrote a long list of all that would be entailed. Top of the list would be the formalities of the house sale.

Our Lincoln house was in joint names and now that Loydz was stuck in Manila because of the UKBA's bone-headed prejudice, it was going to be necessary to send the various sale documents to and from The Philippines for her signature by using regular post, or, more reliably, a professional courier. The first three forms which needed her signature were presented to me by Langleys. These were the contract of sale, the sketch map of the location of the Lincoln house for the UK Land Registry and the transfer document. Langleys sent me the forms by mail. I was told to send them on to Manila for Loydz' signature.

The postal system in The Philippines is not famous for its efficiency or security. Many Filipinos do not use it for sending anything important, which these documents certainly were. I explained the situation to the young woman at Langleys. 'Wouldn't it be better if I scanned in these three documents and sent them by email? They will get there immediately and then we can send them back by courier.'

'No,' the young woman insisted, 'you must send the originals in hard copy.'

'But I can see that they have all come out of a computer. They are in standard Word for Windows format.'

'No, Mr. Payne,' she persisted, with heavy patience, 'they must go as hard copy.'

So, I put them in an envelope and sent them via Royal Mail. I emailed my wife in Manila and warned her to expect them.

'That's the last we'll see of them,' she emailed back. 'Anything from England is going to be stolen, especially if it has things in it which could be valuable.'

And so it proved. After two weeks or so, they had still not appeared at her end. So I got on to Langleys again and explained. This time they were prepared to see reason.

'Yes, just this once, you can scan them in and send them electronically.'

'Do I have to come to your office to get new copies now that the old ones are lost in Manila?'

'No need for that,' the lady from Langleys told me. 'I'll email them to you now.'

Loydz got them five minutes later, and, it still being before five pm in Manila, had them signed and ready for collection by DHL just five minutes after that.

It was about then that I first contacted our shipper, Monkey Removals Ltd., also of Lincoln, to make a start on the packing up. Tim, the man who came to negotiate, turned out to be the boss of the company. He took a fairly cursory look around our tiny semi-detached and said

'Yes, that should be OK. Should all go into a twenty-foot container.'

Containers, for shipping anything from household effects to machinery, come in a range of standard sizes – 20, 40, 60, 80 feet so that the container ships, which may carry thousands of containers per voyage, can be stacked neatly. Each container carries elaborate identifier codes. Since the ship carrying them will make several stops to pick up and unload cargo, there is also a complicated way of loading the ship so that the time spent unloading and loading at each stop is minimised. There is also a complex optimum way of loading the containers not only to ensure minimum time loss at intermediate destinations but also to make sure that the overall weight is evenly distributed for safety in transit. Tim explained to me that the costs would be about £4000 and he subsequently presented me with a quote for £4035. All-inclusive, door-to-door. Payment, naturally enough, since I would be skipping the country, would need to be in advance.

Much of my efforts at the time were devoted to raising the next tranche of money for Vic the Builder, who would be expecting payment of one million pesos at the start of November. By hook or by crook, we managed to find the money in good time. We were, I regret to say, a couple of days late for the November 1st deadline but Vic was quite understanding since most of his men would not be working for the first few days of November anyway. November 1st, All Saints Day, is an important Philippine holiday, stretching over the long weekend and into the following week.

We had now been involved with the selling process for a couple of months without much progress. I phoned Brown's, the estate agents.

'How long is it going to take?' I asked Sarah, the very obliging young woman on the front desk.

'How long is a piece of string?' she replied, and went on to explain that house purchase in England can take anything from two weeks to four or five months. I suggested that we set a completion date for the whole deal at November 30th, with exchange of contracts at or about November 20th.

'Good luck,' said Sarah, 'I'll talk to Langleys.'

I got back to Tim of Monkey Removals and accepted his quote for the shipping and we agreed to stay in touch and arrange payment sometime in mid-November, with final packing towards the end of that month. Loydz was sending me lists of what I would need to buy in the UK for shipment . These included various gifts for her family and friends, which are called '*pasalubong*' in Tagalog. A *pasalubong* is a gift brought from afar and it is considered good manners for foreign travellers to remember their nearest and dearest by such offerings. So, I made several trips to the local Lincoln Tesco to buy both *pasalubong* and articles which are unobtainable or difficult to find in The Philippines. The long list included green tea, dried herbs and spices, chocolates, wine, olive oil and muesli. I also went down to the DIY supermarket to buy a selection of seeds – vegetables, herbs and bulbs for croci, daffodils, tulips etc. Not that I intended to do any gardening myself in my retirement exile. These were all for my wife, who does not share my loathing of horticulture.. Had I known more about the subject I might have realised that the bulbs are all cold-weather species which will not grow in the tropics, something which was subsequently pointed out to us by the several Lipeña landscape gardeners when they visited our finished house to offer their services.

When we did eventually get our building site turned into a garden by a professional landscaper, I completely separated myself from the operation, merely setting Loydz a budget and telling her to get on with it.

This is strange, is it not, for an Englishman to hate gardening? But I justify my detestation of it by reflecting that we, the English, spend too much time attending to the needs of our gardens and the never-ending struggle to maintain their neatness and tidiness. And for what? Walk along any English suburban street and you will see manicured lawns and geometrically precise flower beds as if in a cemetery, all of which are the result of ceaseless and meticulous attention. The only thing you never see in an English garden are human beings. This is because the English climate, for most days some variation of cold, wet or windy, does not lend itself, save for a few days a year, to outside living. The English, for most of the year, live indoors with central heating and warm clothing. How absurd then, this English gardening obsession! Gardens in warm countries – the tropics or the Mediterranean where one can stay outdoors for long periods of time without succumbing to hypothermia, are, sensibly, left to grow naturally, without constant tidying. The only reason I can think of for the English gardening disease is that it represents, to a puritan culture, a year-round opportunity for self-flagellating penance.

The alternative hypothesis might be that the species *homo britannicus suburbanus* is somehow in some kind of symbiotic deadlock with the species garden and he hasn't twigged yet that it is the garden which is using him and not the other way around.

One final duty before my shopping was complete and that was a trip to one of our favourite haunts, Unique Auctions, where there is a monthly auction of antique furniture. In three years of living in Lincoln, we had rarely missed a month. Our house had been too small to allow us to buy much but there were some things we would have liked, for which we hadn't had room. These included an office desk, another couch and a dressing table. The auction on the last Sunday of October was selling a nice Edwardian chaise-longue, which would look good at the foot of our bed, and a leather-topped office desk of the sort I had long coveted. I decided that, with Loydz' agreement, I would bid for them both when they came up late in the afternoon. Loydz at first vetoed the idea and after staying at the auction until lunchtime, I went home. There, waiting for me, was an email from her, saying that she had now viewed the photographs of the two pieces on the Unique Auction website and that she now liked them. So I immediately got back in the car to return to buy them. We got both items together for the bargain price of £200. I love antiques auctions. Why people buy contemporary furniture of inferior quality at vastly higher prices has always been a mystery for me, when excellent antiques can still be picked up for a song. Plus, of course, there is the enjoyable detective work of searching them out.

Four

By the start of November the plan was set. The date for completion of the Lincoln house sale was agreed by Langleys to be the end of the month. The shippers would come to pack up on November 27th and 28th and I would move into a hotel on the 28th. Final completion on the 30th would be when I would receive the funds from the sale and settle up the final tranche of building costs in Lipa.

Langleys confirmed all these arrangements and sent another set of forms for me and Loydz to complete and sign. They consisted of a detailed inventory of the fixtures and fittings which we would be leaving behind – things like lampshades, curtain rails, light bulbs and electric sockets. Amazingly, the lawyers informed me, there are people who will strip a house down to its bare essentials and pack up even the light switches. I find such miserliness difficult to understand. Apart from the natural wish to buy new in a new house, cheapness and meanness are, for me, the most unattractive of traits. Penny-pinching is a strange and counter-productive activity.

While most would hold that the old saying 'penny wise and pound foolish' does contain a kernel of truth, the mere careful hoarding of small amounts of money or inexpensive items works against the grain of good financial husbandry. In my experience, poverty and miserliness are often found together. Meanness is a natural reaction to poverty, of course, but I have met misers who could not claim to be poor but who, nevertheless, lived as though they were. As a result, they were often hard up and, what is more, they lived cramped and mean-spirited lives. On the other hand, people in similar circumstances, those who took a more generous view of their goods and possessions and were happy to pass on, at minimal cost to themselves, those possessions they no longer had use for but which others could be able to use to save cost, time and effort, would prosper. It is a strange paradox whose mechanics I do not fully understand but whose empirical truth I have often witnessed that generosity often creates

Dreaming of England and the lovely snow!

The workers live on site, so first they need a bunkhouse

prosperity but niggardly tight-fistedness frequently leads to financial hardship. The opposite of what one might expect.

I took the Langleys forms about which curtain rails or window blinds or radiator shelves or fitted carpets or pelmets we would be shipping across the world and filled it in as open-handedly as possible. The woman from Langleys asked me if I were sure about the fitted stairs carpet. The previous occupant of the house had taken her stairs carpet. Maybe it is a British tradition. Laying a new one was almost the first thing we had done when we had moved in three years previously. But no, I assured Langleys, we will be leaving all the carpets and all the window blinds and all the electrical outlets.

Once again I was told that the forms would need to be sent in hard copy for Loydz' verification. I pointed out that the far more important contracts of sale had been sent electronically even if their return from Manila was by *über*-expensive commercial courier. And why hadn't all the forms been presented together so that the courier costs would not be duplicated? After a few telephone exchanges, it was agreed that I could fill out the form for both of us and only if the buyer's lawyer raised any questions would it be necessary to obtain a written declaration from my wife that she agreed with my assessment that no, we would not be laying our old fitted carpets from England on our new tiled floors in The Philippines.

I drew up a schedule of what needed to be done. (I have included a checklist for potential émigrés in Appendix C.) One needs to do this and stick to it. I recommend using a spreadsheet, a tool I have found invaluable for domestic administration. With a month to go, I started to contact utilities suppliers, insurance companies, pension providers and the local council, plus several others.

There is a logic in doing this early. Most of the big outgoings, e.g. payments for electricity, water or council tax are, these days, paid online by direct debit. In most cases, these organisations do not want to lose clients and therefore make it difficult to cancel their services when you no longer need them. So most will provide an online form which one must fill up and send out into the ether. Then one has to wait until the following month to see whether they had stopped taking money out of your account because direct debits cannot be cancelled by the payer, only the payee.

About half of my payment cancellations were ignored and I had to make follow-up phone calls, and, in the case of my council tax, a personal visit to Lincoln City Hall, before I could stop the payments. In most cases, the instalments are front-loaded through the financial year so that I was also due a refund. Naturally, most organisations do not like giving refunds, so, in several cases, the phone calls, emails and online forms also had to be supplemented by hard-copy letters. In two cases, I had to resort to threats of legal action.

It was in anticipation of this sort of struggle against the various bureaucracies that I had deferred my departure from England. I knew that I would be spending a lot of time after the house sale had been completed in just following up these loose ends and trying to secure refunds of my overpayments which amounted to several hundreds of pounds. My worst experience was with Sky, who had provided us with telephone, TV and Internet broadband. Their website gave no indication of how one could cancel a contract with them although it was quite fulsome when it came to informing you how one could purchase more of their 'services'. I finally tracked down a phone number near Glasgow and, after being passed from person to person about six times, I finally got through to a man who would be able to cancel some, but not all, of my contract on the due date. I would, he told me, need to write in to another department, whose address he did not have, if I wanted to cancel my Internet broadband. I have never had to cancel a contract before, he bewailed.

Sky were still raiding my bank account right up until the end of January 2013 after I had been resident in The Philippines for a month. Threats of going to OFCOM, the British communications industry regulator, finally got them to agree that I no longer lived in the UK and that I was no longer using their services. They reluctantly gave me a refund of 25% of what they had overcharged me and sent me one of those patronisingly smarmy emails asking me what they had done to deserve my breaking with them.

I also finalised the agreement with the shippers. Tim the Shipper from Monkey Removals came round to the house in mid-November to collect the payment in advance. The £4035 just about maxed out my VISA card. I also changed the arrangements for my pensions, to having them paid to my new account at HSBC instead of Barclays. All these changes went through smoothly although I couldn't help wondering why they mostly required a written letter even though the payments were always made electronically. I also informed my two professional societies, The Institute of Mathematics and its Applications and the British Computer Society, in both of which I have corporate membership, as well as my previous publishers, Authorhouse Inc., who pay me a few pounds royalties from time to time.

Now I was ready to start packing up. I had bought boxes and string and bubble-wrap and brown paper aplenty. The sheer magnitude of my possession mountain was overwhelming. On every previous move, and my wife and I had lived in five countries since marrying in 2006, we had thrown stuff out. On the move to Lincoln in 2009, for example, I had thrown away about three quarters of my library, maybe a thousand volumes. When we had left France that year, we donated innumerable household items to the French incomers. And even though I had first gone to Heidelberg in 2004 with a carload, by the time we were leaving Heidelberg in 2006, our German goods were moved to storage in two Ford Transit vans. The only possible explanation for this inexorable growth in personal possessions is they reproduce themselves so prolifically that no amount of systematic thinning out has any effect on their frantic breeding cycle. I did consider trying to sell off some of the more interesting items via eBay or at the local auction but the sheer effort involved for minute returns, coupled with the knowledge that our 20-foot container would take everything we had and more besides, meant that it was easier just to load most of the stuff into the van. Even so, there was still plenty for the municipal rubbish dump.

The packers duly arrived on the due date. I had very carefully packed up all our clothes, books, office contents, personal bits and pieces, the contents of my two sheds and much of the kitchen. The head packer was unimpressed.

'It'll all have to be re-packed,' he said.

'Why?'

'Got to be made safe. Packed securely so nothing rolls around or gets broken.'

'So, I wasted my time, then.'

'Yes, you did. You should always leave it to the professionals. What's in those?'

'Books. I labelled them.'

'They'll all have to be re-done. Boxes too big. Too heavy.'

So, over the next two days, the Head Packer, assisted by a changing group of Under-Packers, repacked all my packed possessions into different boxes and very carefully, as we found out weeks later when we eventually got them back, rearranged the contents into a pattern which was logical only to a packer. So, books shared boxes with underwear, pictures and kitchenalia, Clothes and pottery were mixed up promiscuously and our DVD's found a common temporary home with wine and socks. Very expertly, for the legion of packers on the strength at Monkey Removals is nothing if not expert, the keys to our largest piece of storage furniture, a very large French sideboard, were carefully hidden away. So well hidden were they that we despair of ever finding them, which means that we are now in the position to offer a very interesting professional challenge to any Filipino locksmith we might be lucky enough to meet. If indeed, such a person exists.

Another variant on the breeding of inanimate objects also presented itself during the packing operation i.e. the well-known phenomenon of the sudden profusion of coat hangers. Thousands of them! I can be quite sure that neither I, nor anyone I know, has ever been into a shop to buy a coat hanger. I have never even seen a coat hanger shop. Where do you go to buy the things? Are they a naturally occurring species being cultivated on vast coat hanger plantations where they grow like Japanese knotweed? Or could there be a huge secret coat hanger cave where Snow White and her Seven Thousand Dwarves are turning them out by the million?

The late John Peel, a famous British radio and TV celebrity, had an interesting theory about the way coat hangers are slowly filling up the universe. He linked the growth in coat hanger population to the related and well-observed phenomenon of putting pairs of socks in the laundry and getting fewer pairs back plus some odd unpaired socks. His theory, which deserves serious consideration in the absence of anything better, is that the odd socks are coat hangers in larval form. The discarded odd socks and those which just disappear will eventually emerge from the Earth as new coat hangers. In the end, the millions of coat hangers were put in the shipment with all the other stuff where they shared boxes with my wife's collection of dried herbs, our wedding photographs, bathroom mirrors and my shoes.

My own visceral aversion to all things horticultural has meant that, over the years, I have shunned garden centres like the plague. One of my several alternative visions of hell is to spend eternity in one. But, given the almost sacred obligation on an Englishman to maintain a tidy garden, as if tidiness were a cardinal virtue ranking far above godliness, charity and faith, I had cravenly succumbed to the silent peer pressure of my neighbours as I had tried to convince myself that it would be better not to risk eternal damnation by refusing to do anything about my little square of *rus in urbe*. The front patch was not much of a problem, being paved over as hard standing for the car. Even so, as my neighbours would helpfully and frequently point out, the weeds which grew thickly, and seemingly instantly, between the paving stones need regular tedious removal with chemicals and a pointed tool.

As for our holy duty to keep the back part tidy, we had paid a local man, Malcolm, to attend once a week, where, for a few pounds he would relieve us of our social and moral obligations.

Thus, we had had only a minimal involvement with the English suburban religion. Nevertheless, and I have no idea how it happened, we had still managed to accumulate much of the paraphernalia of the cult in the form of a lawn mower, a hosepipe, rakes, hoes, spades, shears, a wheelbarrow, various hand tools and assorted nameless gardening bits and pieces. Disposing of these proved simpler than I had feared it would. Dear Malcolm took the whole lot as a parting gift, and even gave the lawn a free haircut in return.

Figuring that the move to Lipa would be the terminal move in a life deeply scarred by numerous changes of address, I was hoping that the experience of living in what might very well prove to be my final home, should not be ruined by having to garden. As it happens, we do have a garden and a nice one. It was installed by a professional landscape gardener called Myla and it is maintained by my wife. I have resolutely refused even to learn the names of the plants which grow in it.

After the packers had stripped the house bare, I called my regular cleaner, Helen, to give it one last scrub and then I spent my first night in the hotel. The next day I returned to dispose of all the material which I was throwing out, although we don't say 'throwing out' anymore. It is now politically correct to refer to the process as 'recycling'. We felt this should be something the local authority could help us with. After all, we had been spending a hundred pounds a month with Lincoln City Council on their 'services', whatever they are. If, that is, they amount to anything more than collecting rubbish once a week, the only thing we ever got in return for our money.

And it was not just any old rubbish they would collect. Oh no, the local dustbin men are now contracted out and privatised, and, as befits a commercial concern, they are very picky indeed about what sort of rubbish they will take. It must not be too big, or made of the wrong material or not on some secret list of prohibited objects or not made from some forbidden material. If it does not suit the fastidious tastes of the privatised bin men, or as they may well be calling themselves these days, 'environmental management consultants', then they will reject it and tell you to make your own arrangements to dispose of it. Which means that you must find another private company who will charge you an arm and a leg to rid you of the offending item. There used to be a famous northern English expression 'where there's muck, there's brass' (*translation* – 'where there's rubbish, there's money'). Never was that truer than in today's environmentally-obsessed Britain.

What to do then with the load of useless rubbish in my sheds – wood, old plant pots, bits of worn-out this and that - which the environmental management consultants would not take in their weekly bin collection? I phoned Lincoln City Hall. The phone was answered after about fifteen minutes.

'Lincoln Council. Helping to create a better Lincolnshire. This is Nicky. How can I help?'

'Rubbish collection? I don't know. I'll put you through to the Environment.'

Another ten minutes later I was talking to another Sarah/Nicky/Jane from the council's Environmental Division.

'No, we don't do collections anymore. Except the weekly. If they won't take something you have to dispose of it yourself. In an approved site of course.'

'Don't you have a municipal rubbish dump?'

'I'll find out. Please hold.'

Ten minutes later she was back.

'You can take rubbish to the tip at....' She mentioned a location on the other side of the city.

'You are not allowed to dump chemicals or anything dangerous but it is free. You have to arrange transport yourself. If you don't have your own transport and you are over seventy or registered disabled, the transport costs are recoverable via social services.'

I loaded up my car five times that day and drove to the tip where there was a sort of small ring road with little stations labelled with various rubbish categories such as 'Cardboard – small', 'Cardboard – large', 'Paper – general', 'Paper – newspapers', 'Glass - bottles', 'Glass - flat' and so on.. The largest and most used station was labelled 'General Landfill' for anything which was otherwise uncategorisable. My betting is that general landfill is where everything would finish up anyway. I have long suspected that much of the religious fervour over the dogma of eco-friendly recycling environmentalism is nothing more than a business opportunity for owners of tracts of otherwise unusable waste land and their friends in the town halls.

I got to the Ibis Hotel on the outskirts of Lincoln by mid-evening. I was surprised to find how tired I was. I ate a sandwich and fell asleep before 8pm. Next day was Friday, November 30th, D-Day for our house sale. I phoned the estate agent and the lawyers, Langleys. They assured me that all was in order and the sale was complete. The funds would be deposited later that day.

Jemma at Langleys gave me again the advice I had been given weeks before when the sale adventure had been starting. Do not, she told me, hand over the keys until the money is safely in your account. This was very interesting to hear. We had spent three months working at this long sale. At every step of the way, two sets of lawyers plus countless estate agents, financial services providers, land registry officials and town hall clerks had been beavering away to ensure that every inch forward was conducted with scrupulous attention to the letter of the law. And now here was a lawyer from the city's top law firm warning me that I could still be cheated, even at the very last minute!

I wasn't cheated, of course, although I was careful to hold on to the enormous assemblage of keys until I could read via my online bank account that we really had been paid. The money came through at noon, or 8pm Manila time. I rushed down to the bank immediately to transfer the final £30,000 or so to Loydz in Manila to pay Vic's men who had been working steadily for a month to the point where our new house now had a roof. The payment would be late of course, after the three days it would take for the transfer to clear and for it to be converted from pounds to pesos.

Engineer Vic would be paying his employees on Saturday as is the custom in The Philippines. Like all builders, as we found out, Vic had a periodic cash flow problem. In my long experience, housing developers are natural multitaskers and always have several projects on the go at any one time. For them, cash flow problems are a way of life. Indeed, cash flow problems and housing developers go together like, well, Burke and Hare or gin and tonic. I was already sanguine about cash flow problems – they had been a feature of my life ever since we had started on this adventure. But I had done my best and so had Loydz. Now, the worst was over and we could see the finishing line.

* * *

Five

By the beginning of December, the Lipa house was taking great shape. Vic's boys had been working overtime. They were largely itinerant workers from the provinces, come to the city, which, like all cities, has sidewalks paved with gold, to find peso-generating work. They lived rough in the bunkhouse from where they ventured out to start work at daybreak, working through until nightfall. Only on Sunday did they cease their labours.

The location of our lot was at the edge of the subdivision, some distance from the gates and the main road running past them. Clearly development of the subdivision had started many years before because the houses near to the road were matured and were starting to need updating.

The banana plants and palms in their gardens had grown higher than their rooftops. As one moves further out, the spaces between the houses become wider, with many empty lots in-between. These lots are still to be sold or may be awaiting their owners' return from exile with the money needed to build a retirement residence. Some of the houses are huge, palatial even. Ours stands modestly, but elegantly, among them.

At the very edge of the subdivision where we live each house is separated from its neighbour by an expanse of grass which gives the impression of spaciousness and affluence. Ours is, and may stay so for a little while yet, near the very edge of the habited area. Two or three solitary houses lie between us and the uncultivated scrub land of papaya, banana, mahogany and palm trees which goes right up to the far boundary wall. On the other side of the wall are the homes of local people, many of whom find employment with the residents of Base View Homes. The area covered by this gated community is some 400 hectares. Vic the Builder is ambitious that it should eventually become a *'barangay'*, or local authority, in its own right.

Loydz, calling heavily on the assistance of cousin Cosette, was now making regular visits to the site in her role as building project manager.

Mostly the journeys were to building suppliers to buy exactly the right kind of wall tile, or the precise shade of paint. The bus journey from Manila, where Loydz was staying in her old family house, takes about an hour by bus if the traffic is not too bad. To avoid the worst of the gridlock, it is necessary to get a bus early. So Loydz would be up before dawn to get to the bus station by, at the latest, 7am. Waiting until 8am could add an extra hour or more to the trip. Buses in Manila city would be locked into the almost stationary traffic, inching forward at snail's pace. Similarly, the return journey also had to be made before what is known, with universally unacknowledged sarcasm, as the 'rush' hour.

Once at Lipa, she would be met by Cosette at the motorway exit, who would take her to see the latest progress on the house. Then off to a conference with Engineer Vic on the fittings and the day's necessary purchase of tiles, paint or whatever followed by an early lunch and a return to Manila, where she would also be handling the various financial matters arising from my transfer of funds from England. She kept up this punishing routine for the whole of the autumn of 2012, acting as a very strict project and financial manager. Without her persistence at keeping the workers to their schedule, the whole project would have taken so much longer. On December 1st, she handed over the final third of the building costs to Vic the Builder and secured from him a guarantee that the house would be habitable by January 23rd. This would include not just the construction, but also the electrical connections, a water supply with water heaters and usable bathrooms.

It is a feature of builders' time estimates that they are always impossibly over-optimistic. There is a good reason for this, of course. Firstly, it will pacify an impatient client. Far better to tell the buyer what he or she wants to hear. If the client complains later, there is a multitude of excuses which can be deployed to explain the miscalculation. These spring readily to the builder's lips – supply delays, labour shortages, bad weather, problems with the utilities suppliers, even the unforeseen time taken to get every last detail just exactly how Sir or Madam had requested it.

*Three white chickens were slaughtered for good luck.
Well, maybe not so lucky for them*

By December 29th Chateau Payne was nearly built

Vic is a fair builder and a straightforward honest businessman, unlike some in his profession. Those, for example, who will happily tell a client, with a dead-pan straight face, that the reason the water has not been connected is because the bricks of the bathroom had to be sent back and re-ordered, which took a week, I promise you, because they had a porosity of 0.012 which is, as you will know, my friend, well above standard building regulations and you wouldn't want that now, would you, Guv'nor?

Fortunately, my wife, although no expert in matters technical, is quite streetwise at an individual level and has a keen sense of knowing when she is being given the verbal run around. So she would, quite shamelessly, cut through the waffle and tell the builder bluntly that he was falling behind and what was he going to do about it and hadn't she come all this way to see such little progress and hadn't Vic and his boys better pull their socks up? Pronto? It obviously worked and the eventual project 'creep' was not nearly as bad as it might have been. We had been promised substantial completion by December 23rd and occupancy by January 23rd 2013. Not too bad - we spent our first night there on January 27th.

A good test of one's effectiveness at managing builders is how soon they want to wash their hands of you. If you are compliant and uncomplaining, they will only visit you occasionally, because they have nine other jobs on the go and those clients may well be more difficult. But if you make a nuisance of yourself to them they will do the job on the hurry-up just to avoid the verbal punch-ups. According to a building quantity surveyor I once knew, the technique is known in the trade as 'throwing a few expletives in'.

Lest you get the false impression that I am patronising the customs of my adopted country, let me assure you that I am not. I have dealt with builders of all nationalities and their codes, excuses and attitudes are universal. Is there a plasterer anywhere, who, when asked to plaster a perfectly flat wall, will not stare at it fixedly for a good ten seconds before exhaling a deep breath and telling you, 'I dunno, mate. It's difficult. It's going to cost you.' Is there a plumber or electrician in the world who comes fully equipped with all the parts and doesn't have to leave after half an hour to get the right size washer or nut and bolt? Not criticisms, just observations. Pretty good then, in my experience, only a very minor project slippage. Overall, Vic did a very good job. So much so that it was a pleasure to see him at our eventual house-warming party.

Meanwhile, back in England, I was preparing for a long stay in hotels. I needed to be at Lincoln Hospital on December 13th for my eye procedures. I particularly wanted an opportunity to say goodbye to my ophthalmological consultant, Christopher Knapp, a fine doctor whom I had got to know and like.

I had moved into the Ibis Hotel in Lincoln at the end of November. I still had much to do in England apart from going to the hospital. I had intended to stay in an Ibis for the whole of December before my flight to Manila on December 31st. My plan was to stay in Lincoln until after my hospital appointment on December 13th and then transfer to a hotel near Heathrow Airport.

For a tourist city, Lincoln has, or had, a remarkable shortage of hotel accommodation, so I could not book a room over the weekend of December 8th, when Lincoln's famous old Cathedral Quarter holds its annual Christmas Fair. So I moved out of the Lincoln Ibis for that weekend and booked a room in a hotel in Chesterfield, an hour's drive away. Nor could I get into the Heathrow Ibis over Christmas so I had to book into The Premier Inn on the Bath Road, alongside the Heathrow main runway, for the period from December 14th to December 31st.

The first job to be done was to get my little car serviced and inspected. Disposing of our car, which had served us well in Lincoln, was a small regret. It was a bright yellow 2003 Suzuki Ignis which we had bought second hand in 2009. Because of its colour, we had christened it 'Daffodil'. It had had only 23,000 miles on the clock, which after nearly four years, we had advanced only to 31,000, it being used mostly only for short trips. I could have sold it for a few hundred pounds. Indeed, I could already hear in my mind's ear the used car salesman's lament – 'not worth anything really, just scrap value.'

But I had a dear granddaughter, Alice, coming up to seventeen and living in Surrey, who would need as soon as she could learn to drive. With its year's MoT (Inspection certificate in the UK.) and its low mileage, not to mention its impeccable reliability record, it would be an ideal first car for her. I spared no expense in making sure, that when I turned it over to her as almost my last act in England, that it would be as safe and roadworthy as it could be made.

The next job was to try to enter the rarefied world of international banking. I had already moved my pension payments to the HSBC Bank and I needed one more trip to the HSBC office in Lincoln High Street, where a very helpful young lady called Donna was on hand to explain to me once again, exactly how their 'Global View' banking system works. Very well, as it turns out. I can now move money from the UK to The Philippines just like one of those *Wünderkinder* on Wall Street. Donna activated my various accounts and I transferred money to them. To make the whole arrangement multinational, as it were, I would need only to connect up with the main HSBC office in De La Rosa, Makati, something which I did as soon as I got to The Philippines. The HSBC connection has worked well so far and serves my purpose as a bank with branches in both my countries. Not, of course, that I hadn't also been totally charmed by the HSBC's very effective famous TV commercial - that mini-soap opera of the little girl with her lemonade stall - which, by now, must have been seen by just about everyone in the world.

I then made an appointment with my local doctor at Lindum Medical Centre where I asked him to prescribe three months of medicines to tide me over until I could organise a regular supply in Lipa. It is one of the features of the modern world that older people need regular dosages of sustaining medicines to palliate the conditions of ageing. So, I take two or three regular pills, plus eye drops, daily, as well as various supplements, which may or may not work, such as vitamin pills and iron tablets.

For one of these non-prescriptive medicaments, I popped into Holland and Barrett, High Street herbalists, to buy three years' supply of saw palmetto, which may, or may not - opinion is divided - slow the natural growth of the male prostate. I am an agnostic when it comes to herbal medicines. On the one hand, they could be little more than expensive snake oil or useless placebos. But, on the other hand, real doctor-prescribed medicines are usually derived from naturally-occurring plants - aspirin from willow being the classic example. So I stocked up on herbal prostate pills of unproven efficacy on the better-safe-than-sorry principle, while simultaneously reflecting that the numerous women buying expensive herbal beauty products were not exactly in the first rank of feminine pulchritude. But then, it may be that H&B beauty products take time to work and they might, indeed, eventually turn these ugly sisters into desirable Cinderella's. If they buy enough of them, I suppose.

During this time, the month of December 2012, I was living out of my car. For years I had travelled around Europe in a former teaching job and I was quite used to treating my car as a second home. My little Suzuki was piled high with all my unshipped possessions including two cartons full of my old shirts and underwear and blue jeans which would be getting their final outings. After I moved out of one hotel and into another I carefully packed up all my dirty clothes into a plastic bag and took them round to the back of the hotel to where their large trash hoppers are parked. The system worked well enough although I underestimated slightly the quantities I should have packed. But my miscalculations were easily put right by trips to Primark, where one can buy disposable clothes imported from Bangladesh at prices not seen at Marks and Spencer since the 1960's.

While staying at the Chesterfield Ibis, I took the opportunity to visit my sister and her husband in Stratford where I enjoyed a very pleasant day out. I managed to get lost twice on the way there and twice on the way back. I must be getting old but I completely missed the signs in the murk and gloom of an English winter's evening. In the last few years, and I can't remember reading about it in the newspapers or hearing it mentioned on the telly, but all the British road signs seem to have been taken away and replaced with much smaller, dimmer ones. After a trip around the suburbs, I found myself going round and round the inner Birmingham Ring Road. I tried to console myself with the fact that there were no whitened skeletons lying beside the road so I could be sure that it was not usual that people would have to spend the rest of their lives there. Eventually I found an exit and by, probably, divine intervention, I was able to escape the deathly grasp of the Birmingham road system and find the M6 motorway.

I also spent some of the time in packing review copies of my two published books with covering letters and sending them to every book reviewer and film producer whose address I could find on the computer. After my visit to the doctors and Mr Knapp, I moved from the north to London and the Premier Inn, Heathrow.

From the London hotel, I was able to visit my daughter and granddaughters who live just south of London and to take some family items to my other granddaughter Mia. I also was able to visit my brother twice. Sadly, he had been hospitalised after a serious setback following chemotherapy. It was distressing to see him so sick but, shortly after my second visit, he had a sudden improvement in his condition and was discharged. I continue to worry about him. The hospital he was in was the first-class Kings College Hospital in Camberwell, South London. I took great pleasure in going there by bus, using my old person's bus pass as issued to me by Lincoln City Council and valid for free off-peak bus travel across the whole of the UK. A wonderful privilege!!

Living in the Premier Inn at this time meant that I spent Christmas Day there. All my family were going somewhere for Christmas so I was on my own. The staff of the hotel were still kept busy as this is an airport hotel and airports don't close at Christmas. Besides, few of the staff and probably fewer of the guests seemed to be British, save maybe for a couple of party girls doing discreet but desultory business in the main lounge. By Christmas Day I had been in the Premier Inn for ten days and I was making a second round of the dinner menu. But they did provide me with a paper hat and the wine list was good. It is not the first time I have had to spend the holiday alone.

On my penultimate day in England before I got the Malaysian Airlines flight to Kuala Lumpur and then Manila, I went to see my daughter,

Alexandra, and my granddaughter, Alice, to hand over the car, which was now empty of all my stuff. They drove me back to Heathrow from their home near Guildford. I ate dinner, slept early and got the shuttle bus to Terminal Four.

Unfortunately at the check-in, I was overweight by some ten kilograms. Here I made another of my characteristic mistakes when they sent me to the 'Repacking Area' to redistribute my luggage by, for example, moving my laptop computer to my carry-on bag. It made not a jot of difference to the overall weight that would have to be carried by the aircraft but now I was only four kilograms overweight, for which they charged me £200! What I ought to have done was to have jettisoned less than that value of my possessions so as to bring the weight down to the required 20 kilos. If I had thrown out the computer printer (five years old and costing only £30 new) and a pair of shoes which I would not need anyway in the tropics and maybe one or two odd bits and pieces, I could have saved myself all that money and bought new in Manila. But it was early in the morning and, at an airport, one undergoes levels of stress at which thinking straight becomes a problem. The beginnings and endings of journeys by air are truly infernal experiences. Maybe they are deliberately made so in order to take the traveller's mind off the fact that cramming hundreds of people into a thin fragile tube and propelling it at very high speeds across thousands of miles through the stratosphere is not a natural condition for our species.

* * *

Six

I arrived in Manila at two in the afternoon on New Year's Day 2013. The long flight from London to Kuala Lumpur was in a new A380 double-decker Airbus. The designers of this huge aeroplane have certainly learnt how to stuff in the cattle, sorry, passengers. I could not see any more toilets in the A380 than in older, smaller planes, which seems to be a design detail they may have overlooked. It would be humane to add some extra provision in this department to compensate for the 30% of toilets which were already out of order when we had left London. I merely offer this as a suggestion to the aircraft designers at the Airbus Corporation should they ever read this book. On the other hand, one could rest one's brain with an excellent selection of movies. Another big plus point is that Malaysian Airlines catering is above normal airline standards, or perhaps it just tastes better because it is served by the world's most beautiful stewardesses.

I slept for most of the four hours on the near-empty connecting flight from KL to Manila where the arrival had none of the usual long waits in line. Even the band which usually plays for incoming passengers to Manila was not on duty. The airport had a holiday feel about it and I was at the Immigration Desk in moments. They had changed the immigration rules slightly since I had last been in Manila in 2008. Incoming passengers needing a three-week temporary visa would now need to show their return ticket as evidence that they did not intend to overstay their welcome and so become a charge on the Philippine state. I did not have a return ticket, so I explained to the immigration clerk what I intended. I showed her my marriage certificate and told her that I was intending to apply for residency.

'Where is your wife now?'
'I hope she's waiting for me outside.'
'What was the date of your marriage?'
'April 28th 2006.'
'What is your wife's home province?'

'She's from Navotas, Metro Manila.'

'Welcome to Manila, Mr. Payne. The Bureau of Immigration is not open tomorrow. It's a public holiday.'

Just at that very moment, my large suitcase was arriving before me on the carousel. I took that as a good omen.

At Manila's Ninoy Aquino International Airport, there is none of that crowding around the arrivals exit which you see elsewhere. For, no doubt, security reasons, there is a further restricted area once one is through customs and out into the arrivals hall. One must push one's cart across a road restricted to use by taxis and buses only and then descend one of two sloping paths, one for those whose surnames begin with A to M and another for those whose surnames begin with N to Z. It is only at the bottom of these walkways that the general public can wait, and where the taxi-touts and the rickshaw wallahs can ply their trades.

On the whole though, Manila does not have too many of the dodgy street characters who greet incomers to many third-world countries. The street beggars are not so conspicuous and one is rarely troubled by unwanted attentions from street vendors. There are still the taxi boys who will broker a taxi ride in exchange for a few pesos. Indeed, these young men, who appear to operate in teams, can be very helpful, especially at the evening rush hour after a long bus ride had deposited you outside the bus station in Makati. The taxis tend to stay in the middle of the road and cannot see a fare on the sidewalk through the crush of the crowds. The taxi boys will find empty cabs for the would-be traveller. Both the taxi-driver and the tout, naturally enough, prefer to work with expatriates, who tip better. But this is still a large third world city and although the streets in the city centre are safe enough and you will not be mugged in daylight as long as you exercise reasonable caution and stay away from the shanty towns and squatters' areas, it is sensible to take the sort of precautions you might take in New York or London. There are pickpockets here, as everywhere, so it makes absolute sense not to flash your money and to keep your hand on your wallet at all times.

This time I met Loydz on the pathway and she had engaged a private driver to take us to our temporary living quarters in cousin Oswald's condominium, quite near to the airport at Paranaqué. Cousin Oswald, like many Filipinos, is a migrant worker in the Middle East and he had bought the condominium, or condo, as both an investment and as somewhere for his children to live when, in time, they become students in Manila. Now it was vacant and we were grateful for somewhere to lay our heads. We had been hoping that our Lipa house would already be finished after a final spurt from Vic's team, but no such luck.

After a day or two recovering from the flight, I was ready to start a new chapter in my life-long struggle against the species bureaucracy. I prioritised my obligations. Money first, so we made a trip to the HSBC Bank in Manila's financial district, Makati. Although I had set up the British end of the connection by opening the peso accounts from England, using the HSBC International Call Center, I still had to complete the arrangement in The Philippines, which meant a whole morning of activating bank accounts, getting PIN's, debit cards, a cheque book, signing at least a dozen forms, obtaining a security 'device', like a little calculator but limited to displaying seemingly random numbers, and transferring sterling to pesos. I found that I still could not transfer sterling to pesos online by myself directly because of local laws governing money laundering, so the bank teller had to do the exchange manually. It would, I was told, be six months, when I had established sufficient residency qualification, before I could make deposits to my accounts. I had also brought £3000 in liquid sterling, sadly reduced by the £200 I had spent on excess baggage at Heathrow. I was intending to change it in small quantities at one of the many money changers whose little offices line the street opposite the bus station.

Living in the small flat was tolerable but not especially comfortable. The bed was too small for the two of us, so we had to spend alternate nights sleeping separately on the bed and the sofa. The main problem was the claustrophobia. The condo had no ventilation in the main room and it was necessary to use air-conditioning and an auxiliary fan to provide cool air. I have never been very keen on air-conditioning. It tends to be too severe. I would much rather be too hot than have to live in an icy draught. Air-conditioning units also tend to be noisy. The Manila climate in January is not especially tropical. Temperatures rise to a maximum of no more than 32C in the afternoon but quite often the sky is cloudy or there is rain. At these times the temperature falls sufficiently for an Englishman not to be unduly troubled by it.

The flat had no cooking facilities, which was not a problem because there are many eateries in The Philippines to suit all tastes and pockets. We could lunch for as little as P100 (£1.60) each for which we got a dish of sweet and sour chicken at a Chinese pavement cafe at the local shopping mall. We paid about P500 each at an OK Japanese restaurant in Makati. At the other end of the scale, costs would come in at P1500 per head including a bottle of Retsina at the Greek restaurant in the Mall of Asia or about the same price at Illustrados, a posh caff in the quaint old Intramuros district.

The condo, in addition to its lack of ventilation, also lacked hot water or facilities for washing clothes. In a hot country, one takes frequent showers but after a short time of adjustment, we got used to showering in cold water. (Shades of my schooldays!) As for clothes washing, Loydz devised a program of returning to her old family house where her maid, who doubled as companion to her elderly mother, would receive the clothes and return them, washed and ironed, a few days later.

Travelling around Manila is cheap and easy. There is a range of options for those not brave enough, or stupid enough, to risk driving themselves. The traffic is horrendous, with little regard for driving conventions as practised in the west. But the taxi drivers are adept at squeezing in and out of traffic and exploiting every minute advantage to push into any space in order to gain a little progress. Road usage in the whole country is ungoverned by attention to good manners or even personal safety.

Road users from single pedestrians right up to the heaviest juggernauts consider themselves of equal importance. They do not need to pay attention to their own safety, since it is the obligation of other road users to avoid them. Even young children will amble slowly across a busy highway without bothering to turn their heads to the direction of the oncoming traffic. There are police around, but they take little interest in managing the traffic flow, except, occasionally, to do a little ineffectual point duty if the mood takes them. As far as I could tell, most drivers take little notice of the police hand-flapping. I always have to ask Loydz what each of the policeman's had gestures means. 'Go, just go!' she always replies, whatever the hand signals from the policeman. Traffic in The Philippines behaves exactly as it would if the country were governed on strict anarchist principles of individual responsibility. Quite unlike the highly controlled and regulated system as pertains in Europe or North America.

For someone scared by this individualism, as I am, there are other options. Taxis are cheap and plentiful in Manila, although not in Lipa, the first city I have ever lived in which does not have a taxi service! In Manila, the ride from Paranaqué into the city centre, a journey of a few kilometres, would only cost about P120 (or £2 or $3). A couple of times we had to visit our shipper out at Taguig on the edge of the metropolis. The journey there and back, plus a fifteen minute wait took two hours, which set us back a whole P500 (including a 10%tip) which amounts to less than nine pounds sterling.

For the local people who must travel around the city regularly, there are the jeepneys. These street buses travel everywhere and can be hailed like a taxi. They are low, brightly painted vehicles with two long benches. One enters at the rear and finds a place on the bench. The fare – here in Lipa, it is a standard P8 for short journeys in town – is passed over the heads of the other passengers to the driver. As one approaches one's destination, one shouts to the driver, who stops just long enough for you to jump off. Jeepneys are safe during the daytime but they are best avoided after nightfall. Loydz' bag was slashed and her purse stolen when riding in a jeepney in central Manila after dark. For westerners, who look rich and muggable, they are best only used when accompanied by a streetwise Filipino. For very short journeys there are the tricycles, motorised or pedal-powered. For ten or twenty pesos, one can take a short trip of a few hundred metres through parts where a taxi would not go. In Lipa, the tricycle is the local version of the taxi and costs something like P100 for a journey of a kilometre or so.

We obviously had much to do in Manila and we prioritised our problem solving according by money, house, immigration, shipment. The money problem looked as if was solved, so the next thing to do was to make the trip to Lipa to view progress on the house. Loydz had been going there two or three times a week since October but she could not stand over the workforce continuously and, in reporting back to me, she would often express disappointment at the lack of progress since her previous visit. This would be my first opportunity to meet Cosette, who had done a magnificent job of driving Loydz to and from the building site and also to make the acquaintance of Engineer Vic.

The schedule was now adrift by a month, according to Vic's Gantt charts. But I suppose that is only to be expected. All building projects are behind schedule. It is an inexorable law of nature. Engineer Vic was pleasant, friendly and his excuses were quite plausible. But builders are builders and they must follow the hallowed sacred precepts of their ancient calling. Vic was merely following the time line of builders everywhere. The major part of the construction goes up fairly quickly and the final details, the parts which actually make the house usable - such as windows, water, bathroom, sewerage, electricity - the last 20% of the project - take about the same amount of time as the first 80%.

To get to Lipa from Manila, you take the bus from the Makati bus station. The journey can take an hour or three hours depending on the traffic and the time of day. There are several toll stops along the way and the bus also stops to allow the inspector to get on to check the takings. The cost of a one-way journey is either 89 or 99 pesos depending on which bus company you are using. Actually the bus conductor operates a strange ticketing system. First he goes round the bus issuing tickets which are punched with holes using a code whose understanding would defeat Bletchley Park. Then he comes around again to collect the money, which he does from memory. There is no fixed departure time, which makes sense given there is no fixed travel time either. The bus leaves the bus station, pushing its way through the jeepneys, taxis, pedestrians, trikes and bikes and out into the road, when it is full. Up until that time and for the first half mile or so of its journey, a non-stop stream of street vendors moves up and down the aisle selling peanuts, dried banana chips, sandwiches, bottles of water and who knows what else.

The ride was comfortable enough along the South Luzon Expressway or SLEX and we arrived at Tambo Exit, the dropping off point for Lipa, there to be met by Cosette, who had been waiting with her car, which she had parked at the gasoline station there. First stop, the Cafe Lipa for coffee. The area around Lipa is a coffee bean growing area, and the local coffee is excellent. After the Cafe Lipa it was a trip to the other side of town to see the house.

At that time, the first week of January, the house was still unfinished. A swarm of young men were working on it but progress was not much advanced from when Loydz had visited two weeks previously. We told Engineer Vic that we wanted to start living in it by the end of the month. No problem, it will be ready long before that, he assured us. I have always been suspicious when someone begins a sentence with 'no problem.' It is one of those phrases right up there with 'you can't miss it', 'trust me' and 'you've plenty of time'. In my experience they always mean the exact opposite. Vic even hinted that he was looking forward to receiving the contracted 'hold-back' payment - the last 200,000 pesos of the price which is paid over after the job is completely finished and the new owners are satisfied with the workmanship. We ignored this last hint as builder's traditional cash-flow panic.

There was nothing we could do but to promise another visit very soon and return to Manila. There were other things we had to deal with. One which was starting to trouble us was the location of our household possessions. We began sending frantic emails to Monkey Removals back in Lincoln to try to find out the name of the agent who would be handling the Philippines end of the deal. This was a worry for us because Loydz, via one of her contacts in the Philippine shipping business, had come across a list of local shippers who had been barred from the Manila docks for non-payment of harbour taxes. We had sent Monkey Removals this list with the strong command – do not use any of these companies!

Back at the condo in Manila, we reviewed the state of our problem portfolio. Money transfer problem – just about solved; immigration problem – deferred for a week or so; shipment problem - the onset of panic; house completion problem – working on it but feeling we were pushing at an immovable object. But there was one ray of sunshine. We discovered Gerry's Grill where they serve good food to a trendy, yuppie, Friday night crowd and do a great line in delicious Blue Margaritas at P495 a pitcher!

* * *

Seven

There was no phone line in the condo and, obviously, no Internet connection. It is easy to forget, in this era of Facebook and Twitter just how recently it was that no-one had any electronic communications at all, except for a telephone landline. People only started emailing as little as fifteen years ago and even ten years ago not everyone was online. I had brought my laptop with me from Lincoln. During my stay in the hotels I had found a way of buying Internet space via various deals, expensive – natch - as part of my hotel bill. Here in Manila our problem was similar because it is an unavoidable fact of modern life that one just cannot survive as a social animal without email and the World Wide Web. Not that I use it for social networking of course. At bottom I am a anti-social recluse, or so I have been called, even though I have no criticism of Facebookers. But even I cannot manage my own limited business and social contacts without regular emails. What we had to do in this situation was to buy pay-as-you-go cards for Internet connection. They tend to be expensive at about 100 pesos for ninety minutes online but I found that they would give out within a shorter time than that unless one was very careful to make sure they were properly disconnected after use. The cards were only usable if one had first bought a small USB antenna for a connection which could be either dial-up or wireless broadband.

Unfortunately, the cards were not available except in the larger shopping malls, so one needed to buy a week's supply at a time. This arrangement was clearly inconvenient but essential while we were in the condo. An alternative might have been to use an Internet cafe but there was none nearby. The apartment block which housed the condo did have an Internet room with half a dozen machines but the only one with a working Internet connection was in continuous use by children playing computer games.

One of the first things we did when we finally moved into our new house was to buy a proper contract with a local Internet Service Provider

*By the end of January 2013,
it was completely built and we could move in*

And pretty soon after that, we also had a garden

who supplied a domestic wireless router so that we could run several computers off it simultaneously.

Before moving to Lipa, we spent a day at the Bureau of Immigration where I would need to get my visa before my temporary tourist visa expired on January 21st. The process of securing legal residence status is as convoluted in The Philippines as it is in the UK. It is a three stage process, and the visit we made on January 14th to the Bureau, described in the next chapter, opened our eyes to its myriad complications. I could only think that the Bureau was no more complex than its equivalent, the UKBA, in England.

On January 18th, we made another trip to Lipa. We could see little progress since the previous week. Once again Vic assured us that the house would indeed be habitable by Friday January 25th, only two days later than the original scheduled completion date. As far as we could see, there was internal painting still to be done, cleaning and painting of the stair rail, tiling of the bathroom, installation of the water heaters, fitting out of the kitchen and so much more. We made it clear that we were seriously intending to move in on Friday the 25th and it had better be ready. No problem, said Vic, once again.

On the basis that we still didn't know when our shipment would be delivered, we prepared to live minimally in the new house. We would need some basics such a set of garden furniture, a round plastic table and four chairs which would suffice as regular furniture for the time being, and a sofa bed. Plus basic kitchen equipment, some of which Loydz had already been accumulating. There was a fridge already bought and installed and cooking was possible on a small stove running from a gas tank. So with Cosette's help we bought what we needed at the SM Mall in Lipa, including TV and vacuum cleaner, and we arranged delivery for the following week.

We also bought a car from Winnie, another of Loydz' cousins, which she sold to us for what she described as a 'family price'. It is a large Suzuki people carrier, far too frightening for either Loydz or me to drive on the Lipa roads, which I had come to consider something of a warzone. Buying a car in The Philippines is not a bit like the quick and easy process it is in most countries. It is a long palaver of getting the papers transferred officially. Then the bill of sale must be notarised and the registration document presented to the Motor Vehicle Office in one's home town. Then there is the 'stencil' to be deposited with the authorities. This is a rubbing of the engine number. Finally the insurance must be transferred. Winnie had kindly allowed us to try out this behemoth on a quiet bit of road near Oswald's condo. I am afraid I got a little bit over-confident about my abilities to master any form of motor vehicle in any conditions. I had survived the German Autobahn, where the drivers drive to kill and I had even driven a newly rented car around the Paris *Périphèrique* at rush hour so I, naively, thought that I would have no problem with a car which was much larger than I was used to and which was also automatic (I hadn't driven an automatic in seven years.) What is more, the steering wheel was on the wrong side because right-hand-drive cars are illegal in The Philippines. Winnie kindly drove it to Lipa for us during one of our visits and parked it in Cosette's forecourt.

The house was more or less ready for occupancy, as Vic had predicted it would be, by the weekend of January 25th. Unfortunately, we couldn't get transport for Friday January 25th, but another obliging young man from Loydz' old neighbourhood was willing to drive our belongings to Lipa on Sunday January 27th. On the Saturday, Loydz took me to a street market in Baclaran, near the condo in Paranaqué, to buy curtains and curtain rails. I think buying curtains, as an activity, beats even gardening for dreadfulness but I went along with her and she bought some burgundy coloured drapes and the rails to match. It was my first experience of a real third world street market where one threaded one's way through narrow, muddy, crowded alleyways between stalls selling evil-smelling hot food and places where plastic trinkets and cheap lighters were on sale at baby-money prices plus some stalls whose merchandise I just did not want to investigate.

On the Sunday, we were up very early so that Loydz could go to her old house to pick up her paraphernalia as well as a few of the wedding presents which she had been storing since 2006. These came back with her in the jeepney. Actually, it was not a passenger jeepney, but a cargo jeepney – jeepneys come in two models, with or without seats and windows. Just like jumbo jets.

At Lipa, the jeepney was unloaded, and later Bobi and Cosette came around with our TV and the plastic garden furniture. The sofa bed was already delivered. So we had the basics for living. They also brought Arabella, the new car, named for the husband-murderess in my previous book, 'ERASED!'

In our first few days in the new house, the work on the interior and the exterior finishing was still continuing. When Vic the Builder had told us the house would be habitable by the end of January, he was being only technically correct. During the next few weeks, armies of local workers would be swarming over the house doing painting and cleaning and scraping and drilling and hammering and tiling. Often there would be as many as ten separate operations going on at the same time.

Every morning, we would prepare a 'punch list' of jobs still unfinished or in need of what only might be called 'post-implementation repair', such as the numerous small repaintings which were necessary after a paint job had needed re-doing and had left new splashes on the adjoining area.

We also needed some extra furniture above what was included in the load and we had a computer table and Loydz' dressing table made by a local carpenter - in local mahogany, no less, something prohibitively expensive in the UK. The workmanship was good and the price reasonable.

It was just about this time that we finally found out the name of the company responsible for the final delivery of our shipment. They were called Asian Tigers and worked out of a warehouse complex in Taguig, an outer suburb of Manila, about an hour's taxi ride from the city centre. The container ship, with our furniture on it, would be in Singapore by January 24th, with maybe a week's further shipping time before arrival in Manila.

Asian Tigers, who proved very efficient, sent us a list of all the immigration documentation, seven pieces in all, that we would need before our shipment could be released and delivered.(Appendix D.)

We had repeatedly emailed Monkey Removals in Lincoln as to the name of the company who would be responsible for the final delivery but every time without success. So, it was actually a relief to get their name, even if it hadn't come from Monkey Removals but had been communicated to us by Asian Tigers themselves. Once we knew what Asian Tigers needed, which amounted to evidence that I was a visa-owning, tax-registered, legal resident, we could put our efforts into completing the formal immigration process which we had started the previous week.

* * *

Eight

The Philippines has a large bureaucracy, like most countries. Jobs at city hall or in the utility 'boards' are safe and well-paid by local standards. I can well remember my childhood in Britain's first austerity period, and how desirable it was to have 'a good job at the town hall'. After the Depression and the war which followed it, nothing could be more respectable or attractive than guaranteed, well-paid, lower middle class employment as a clerk or bookkeeper on the municipal payroll. Going to work 'dressed up in their Sunday best', as my father described it, was the acme of ambition for many working-class children, far preferable to stressful, grimy work in the factory or coal mine. In those far-off days, when there was plentiful employment, I remember that our local paper, *The Oldham Evening Chronicle*, would carry numerous adverts in its 'Sits. Vac.' pages for clerks of all kinds – sales clerks, invoice clerks, purchasing clerks, accounts clerks, order clerks - clerks of all types and functions. A clerical job was always available for anyone who could pass the appropriate exams at evening class. All gone now, of course, all those jobs, those lifelines of ambition for the poor but hard-working Joe Lampton's. All swept away by the ubiquitous computer.

But to enter a Philippine town hall or utility office, it is impossible for me not to be overcome by a nostalgia I did not know I was capable of. There they are, all those Filipino clerks with their ledgers and rubber stamps and their in-trays and out-trays with barely a desk-top computer in sight. How wise, I think when I survey the anachronistic scene. How wise of the managers not to allow themselves to be seduced by the dubious charms of 'efficiency' and 'modernisation' and 'productivity'. How wise to continue to do their bureaucratic works manually in the old way, to employ ten people on low wages rather than, as often happens in the west, to employ one well-paid person to do the same work using a computer so that nine others can go unemployed.

Of course, Philippine immigration procedures are long-winded and tedious, with numerous redundant repetitions and duplications. The output of each part of the immigration production line is checked, counter-checked and counter-counter-checked mercilessly. Every piece of paper is notarised and multiply photocopied so that any user of the service will soon amass a vast library of documents. Where the original of an important document, a birth certificate, a marriage contract, the title deeds of one's house, is required, then supporting triplicated photocopies of the same document are sometimes also, needlessly, demanded.

Dealing with any branch of the Philippine bureaucracy, is a glacially slow experience. And, one soon learns, it is better to resign oneself early to its frustrations, lest anger and despair contrive to make the experience even more hellish. But, in my experience, it compares well with bureaucracies in the west which are also slow and inefficient in spite of the western bureaucracies' access to computer networks and the most expensive management consultants. Indeed, most bureaucratic systems anywhere are, in the final analysis, little more than make-work methods for generating economic activity after the manner of Keynes' men digging holes and filling them in again. That all bureaucracies are ultimately fatuous is easily verified. The world is full of illiterates who can neither read the bureaucrat's forms nor fill them in. But nothing stops such people from enjoying a real life and its landmark events of birth, reproduction and death. Indeed, if they are resourceful illiterates they can even make a decent living without first having to get the permission of someone sitting behind a desk at the town hall.

But I was quite happy to go through the hoops of the convoluted Philippine immigration circus, theirs being no more elaborate than those of the UKBA, as well as being both much cheaper and significantly friendlier. So, I embarked on the multi-staged immigration process with the eventual aim of getting permanent settlement in The Philippines if not exactly with pleasant anticipation, then at least with optimistic resignation.

The first stage is the temporary visitor's visa which I had been given at the airport. The next stage requires attendance at the Bureau of Immigration building in Intramuros, Manila. I had been informed that one could wait until near the end of the three week tourist visa period before applying for permission for a longer stay. This turned out to be the wrong advice. I had arrived in Manila on January 1st. What I ought to have done was to have gone down to the Bureau of Immigration immediately, or at least as soon as the jet-lag had started to wear off. Instead I left the visit for two weeks. We went there on Monday January 14th, while we were still living in the condo. Naturally, one does not interface with the world's immigration bureaucracy without first equipping oneself with every possible document describing the entirety of one's life. So we consulted the Bureau of Immigration website where there is posted a list of everything one will need to take including downloadable forms to be filled up and both our passports. Loydz will be my sponsor for immigration and so her credentials would be scrutinised as fiercely as mine. So we would also need to present notarised birth, divorce and marriage certificates properly authenticated by the National Statistics Office. We would also need to provide proof of income, in the form of my pension statements plus bank certificates to show that we are indeed solvent and that we can afford to live in The Philippines. HSBC are used to providing these, which they did immediately and at no cost. (The full list of required documentation is reproduced in Appendix E.)

We got a taxi from the Paranaqué condo to go the few miles to Intramuros in central Manila. As we opened the door at our destination, we were accosted by an army of small and teenage boys touting for custom.

'Custom for what,' I asked Loydz.

'They are,' she explained,' drumming up business for lawyers who are also public notaries. Notarisation is a big business here. Ignore them.'

The main, ground floor office of the Bureau was jam-packed with seething humanity. All nationalities were present and, interestingly, many in religious garb - nuns, mainly. There was a preponderance of Indians and Chinese and several Filipina women carrying sheaves of applications. These would be from the human resources departments of various companies or from travel agencies, who would be processing multiple applications *en masse*. It is the law that every applicant for immigration must be sponsored by a Filipino company or individual, in my case, by my wife, Loydz.

The second stage of the visa process is to get a replacement for the 21-day short visa by another visa, the 9-A, for which is valid for 59 days from the date of first entry. This is so that you will be street-legal while the Bureau processes the third stage – the temporary one-year visa. The applicant must fill out the downloaded form which must be notarised and photocopied. There is a photocopier in the corner of the main office which is running non-stop and for the half-dozen or so photographs which will be needed, there is a freelance photographer doing very brisk business. Fortunately, although one needs copious photocopies and photographs, the costs are minimal. The obligatory notarisation is done by two young women, called, because they have law degrees, 'Attorney', as is the Filipino custom. Why exactly the swarm of young men outside are so busy trying to drum up notarisation trade, is difficult to fathom. These two young attorneys were doing their notarising at full tilt for free. Maybe the boys outside were just trying to catch the naive first-timer who might not realise that Bureau notarisation is included as part of the overall cost of the service? The notarisation trade is just a business like any other. To be sure, there is a little culture shock to see these lawyers' runners grubbing for clients on the street but that differs only in degree from western ambulance chasing. One can be absolutely certain that, in the unlikely event that the bottom were ever to fall out of the lucrative world-wide lawyer's cartel, then even the up-market legal eagles of Wall Street or The Inner Temple would not be above sending out their touts to raise business.

So, having all the papers together for a longer, 59-day visa, one can go the cashier's window and pay. It costs, in all, about P3,500 or approximately US$90 or £60 sterling. Naturally, the windows for doing all these tasks are not next to each other in logical sequence, so one is directed to a window across the hall or at the other end of the building. Having paid for the stamp, it is then back, with the cashier's receipt, to a new window, where one's passport will then be stamped. In my case, the visa was dated up until March 1st. I was now a legal immigrant for the next six weeks.

Having got the 59-day visa, I was ready to move on to the next stage, the application for a 13-A one-year probationary visa. This 13-A visa is the classification for non-quota immigrants i.e. those, like me, applying for residence by virtue of marriage to a Philippine citizen. It is the prelude to obtaining permanent permission to remain. Could the application for a 13-A be made on the same day without having to return? Amazingly, yes! We were first sent away for lunch and told to return in the afternoon. Now we could begin the application for a one-year visa. Again, the same steps of form-filling, notarisation and multiple photocopying were gone through, almost exactly as they had been that morning. We spoke to the same attorneys and we paid our money at the same window. The cost for a twelve-month stamp is, naturally enough, higher than the rate for shorter visas and comes in at P8,620 (approx. US$200 or about £125) plus various odds and ends such as photocopying and photographs. Then I had to make a separate application for the ACR-I card, the Alien's Certificate of Registration Identity card. (With the usual forms, triplicated photocopies, photographs etc.) which costs about P2000 or $50. Part of the cost goes to pay for an investigation by the National Bureau of Investigation to check that the applicant is not a criminal known to the Philippine police.

The next stage was that we were told to come back three days later for the interview with an attorney and for the 'biometrics'. We duly appeared and waited an hour in the attorney's office. The interview was brief. All the attorney was interested in was to ascertain that we really were married and I was a *bona fide* spouse seeking to make a home in The Philippines. He was quickly satisfied with our replies.

'Do you have children together?'

'No, too old,' we told him.

'But still trying, eh?' he leered.

I then went to give up my biometric data. First I was photographed full-face and profile by a digital camera online to one of the rare Bureau computers, one of the very few we actually saw there. But it was connected up to an efficient system which would read fingerprints digitally and produce a comprehensive record – data, photographs and fingerprints, all on a single electronic record. When I had done that I was then sent to the photographer who took a conventional hard-copy photograph in full-face and profile. My fingerprints were then taken again using an old-fashioned ink roller. A sensible precaution, to double up the record-taking. Who would ever trust those new-fangled computer thingies?

On the way out of the attorney's office, his secretary had given us the address of the official Bureau of Immigration website, which, every Monday, publishes under the link 'List of BOC acted applications', the names on all those visa applications which had been granted in the previous week. Our projected date for my 13-A visa approval was February 11th 2013. But we found, to our delight, that my name as applicant, and Loydz' name as sponsor, appeared on the list published online on January 28th. By now we had already moved to Lipa, so we made arrangements to go back to Manila on Wednesday January 30th. I would retrieve my passport with its new 13-A visa stamp. This, the stamped passport, and not just a certified copy, would be needed by our shippers, Asian Tigers, before they could arrange customs clearance of our household effects.

The day of the trip from Lipa to Manila to get my stamped passport from the Bureau of Immigration started out badly. I drove our new car down to the town to park it in the supermarket car park. It was a very frightening experience to be driving it, for the first time, in the morning rush hour.

Driving in The Philippines is not for the faint-hearted. There are no rules of the road, except the one fundamental rule of Filipino driving – 'Don't Hit Anything!' Well, on that first foray out into what I came to think of as the 'warzone', we didn't hit anything. Something hit us.

To get into the car park where we had intended to leave our car while we were in Manila, entailed forcing one's way across the traffic stream. I did that successfully, relying heavily on my vast reserves of vindictive aggression. Unfortunately, once we had got to the car park, it turned out to be closed until the store opened an hour later. I was about to do a three-point turn to go back when a police car parked itself alongside me, making the manoeuvre impossible. So I was forced to reverse back out into the traffic stream and push my way into the traffic going in the opposite direction. It was at this point, when we were stationary and awaiting a gap, that a motor cyclist, going far too fast, decided to drive into our new car on its maiden voyage. Maybe 'Arabella' had not been a good choice of name for our vehicle? Perhaps 'Titanic' might have been more appropriate? Fortunately, the biker was indisputably in the wrong and he drove off before the police, who had been languidly watching the whole episode from their car, could come over to ask him questions. And the fact that he was, hopefully, uninjured, meant that there would be little mileage in trying to extract informal reparation from this blameless foreigner. So the brave custodians of the law merely, and discreetly, looked the other way.

But we were very shaken up and after we had found an alternative parking space and taken a strong coffee. (I really needed a large scotch but alas, none was available.) Even our second choice of parking space turned out to be a mistake. Someone stole our hub caps while we were away. But we got the bus back to Manila for stage four of the immigration saga, the stamping of the passport.

I presented myself and my passport at the designated window and we were told to sit down. Then more forms were filled out and photocopied. These forms and my other documentation were scrutinised by the 'Receiver' whose job it is to receive documents. After some stamping and stapling we were given back the bundle of forms and told to take them to the 'Checker', whose job it is to check that the Receiver has properly received the documents. Then, after more stamping, signing and stapling, we got the growing bundle back again to pass it on to the 'Implementor' whose task it is to check that the Receiver has properly received all the papers and to check that the Checker has correctly checked them. The

Implementor then told us to sit down. After a while she called us over. Would we be getting our visa? Well, no, not yet, come back at 3.00pm. It was now eleven o'clock and so we had four hours to kill.

'What about my Alien's Card?' I asked.

'Five to ten days,' she told me. A vital document is the ACR-I card. Without it, one cannot leave the country, and this being election year when security paranoia is higher than usual, and what is more, me being an obvious foreigner, who knows when I might be required to identify myself to the authorities?

Precisely on the dot of 3.00pm, the deliverer of passports had my passport ready with, at long last, a virgin 13-A visa newly stamped in it. We rushed from the Bureau of Immigration and straight into a taxi to take a ten-kilometre ride to the remote suburb where Asian Tigers have their offices. There we handed over my passport (plus photocopies thereof) and the woman in charge then took numerous photocopies of all the other relevant documents including the receipt for my ACR-I card. I still needed, before the Bureau of Customs would be satisfied, a tax number or TIN. We agreed that we would email this to the shippers as soon as we had it. (See Appendix D for the list of forms etc required by customs.)

Then back to the centre of Manila to find the Bureau of Internal Revenue with the intention of obtaining a tax number. After being misinformed by the taxi driver of the location of the tax office, we were able to waste an hour driving round a crowded inner city trying to find it. It turned out to be the building across the street from the Bureau of Immigration, where we had already spent most of the day. We need not have bothered. As Lipeños, as we are called, we need to get our tax numbers from the local Lipa office. Tax collection is still not centralised, another similarity with 1950's Oldham. We got back home to Lipa, long after dark, when the road driving conditions, dangerous enough by daylight, are even more frightening. But we made it back, alive and in one piece, with only minor damage to our new car.

The next day we got up bright and early for another episode in the struggle. This time we were driven by the ever-obliging Cosette, whose familiarity with Lipa and her unstinting willingness to drive us, is something we will always be grateful to her for.

The Lipa tax office is in the old part of the city where the streets are narrower and more crowded than the main highway - the only road where we felt we had a fighting chance against the other road users. I felt slightly less cowardly when Cosette, a long-time Lipeña, confided that she, too, when she had first got her car, had been too intimidated by the traffic to drive in the old part of Lipa.

There was a line outside the office, but by influence or just by having a dumb foreigner in tow, we managed to get to the front without waiting. Two guards were on duty beneath a sign with the intriguing message 'Thank you for paying your taxes' as if tax-paying were voluntary, like giving to charity. Another sign at the guard post enjoined citizens to 'Please leave firearms with the guard.'

The tax-gatherers at the Lipa tax office were quite friendly and, with the help of wifely translation, I managed to become a member of the tax-paying citizenry. Actually, I am virtually fully retired now, so I don't think I will be paying income or business taxes in my new country. But it was important to be legal for the customs and excise officials or I would never be able to reclaim my worldly chattels, which, at that time, were aboard a container ship somewhere in the South China Sea.

Naturally, a trip to the tax office could not go off without a bit of form-filling. So, I filled in the form – surname, forename, address, and so on.

'Middle name?' asked the clerk.

'I don't have one.'

'But you have to have a middle name. Everybody has a middle name. The form needs one.'

'But I don't have one. My mother didn't believe in middle names.'

'What about your mother's maiden name?'

'If you insist. Her maiden name was Worrad.'

'Fill it in.'

So I wrote my mother's maiden name as my own middle name. I have managed seventy years with just the two names, surname and forename. It comes as a late surprise to have to grow a new name at this point in my life. But what the hell, if that's what they want, who am I to care?

Actually 'Christopher Worrad Payne' has a little bit of pretentious stylishness about it. If I ever make it as a posh writer I might use it as a *nom de plume*. Who knows? I may, in time, even add the flourish of a hyphen. I'll think about that.

We emailed the TIN to our shippers and prepared for stage five. Two weeks later, after confirming that the shippers had obtained customs clearance and therefore no longer needed to retain my passport, we made another trip to Manila to get back the valuable maroon little booklet and to pick up the ACR-I card. Amazingly, getting the card from the Bureau of Immigration was the easiest part of the whole process. I went straight up to the desk – no queue – showed my passport and the receipt and the ACR-I card was handed over. Total time? - five minutes.

Actually, the process as I have described it, was no more difficult than dealing with other immigration bureaucracies and a good deal easier than most. As I have said, the British UKBA is misleading, perverse, obstructive, unfriendly and expensive. But there are others which are nearly as bad. And we regularly found Turkish immigration officials to be particularly difficult and obtuse. The best immigration experiences have been with Spanish, French and German, and now the Philippine bureaucracies, all of which have proved helpful on those occasions when we have come into contact with them.

However, I did do some things wrong. The first mistake I made was to enter the Philippines via a tourist visa. The long process of conversion of the 21-day visa, first to a 59-day visa and then a year-long probationary visa could have been circumvented if I had applied for my 13-A visa directly from the UK. I could have speeded up the whole process if I had made my application via the Philippines Embassy in London. So, while I was in the process of packing up in England, my visa application could have been proceeding in parallel.

Another mistake I made was to delay the application.. There is no advantage in waiting. I should have gone straight to the Bureau of

Immigration as soon as I was able to. By not doing, we worried unnecessarily about getting the immigration approval in time to get our shipment. We thought that we would be running up port storage costs while waiting for visa approval to come through. This would have also required us to put up a bond to cover the possible cost of sending our shipment back to the UK. In the event, though, we need not have worried. As it happened, customs clearance was the slowest part of the whole emigration experience. But it would have made sense to have done as much as we could while we were still living in Manila and before we moved into the new house in Lipa.

I should also have looked at other visa options. There is, for example a Special Resident Retirement Visa or SRRV for those not sponsored by spouse or their company but who wish to retire to The Philippines independently. Emigrants in this category need to put up financial guarantees. By all accounts, the processing of a SRRV is much easier and faster than that for a 13-A. (Appendix E)

I have, of course, dealt with paper-heavy bureaucracies before and, like many, I have often wondered where all those paper records eventually finish up. A friend of mine, someone used to living in countries with bureaucracies where vast quantities of paper are consumed like elemental cosmic matter in a black hole, tells me that the offices must sit on top of a vast network of tunnels wherein all the memos and ledgers are eventually stored for the benefit of future archaeologists. This theory is plausible but unlikely since the mere maintenance of this vast storage scheme would itself require a large bureaucracy of its own, with a corresponding grandiose management superstructure to oversee it and there is no evidence of that.

No, the great paper machine is just a small part of the nature's grand design. The mighty paper-bureaucracies of the world not only provide much-needed economic activity in poorer countries, but they also play their role in controlling the ecology of the planet - keeping the world 'green'. In a very short time, today's vital, must-have, live-or-die piece of paper will decompose and be recycled. For unlike the indestructible microchip and the plastic boxes of modern information technology, which will stay intact, with their data, for the rest of eternity, the mountain of paper in an office like the Philippines Bureau of Immigration is no more than the temporary manifestation of the elements of which it is composed. The paper state of these elements is a mere ephemeral, temporary transitional form, before the paper returns to its primary chemical components which will subsequently be reincarnated as yet another tree, ready to be turned into new reams of A4 (or bond paper as they call it here) in a never-ending cycle.

In fact, it is even better than that. Those misguided environmentalists, who want to recycle paper using nasty chemicals, in order to 'save the planet', do not seem to realise that the alternatives to paper, the use of even nastier chemicals and primary fossil resources to construct the instruments of 'paperless' information technology, are far, far worse. Using more paper forces the lumber companies to grow more trees, usually fast-growing prolific softwoods - never expensive tropical hardwoods, that is another issue - which inhale and 'fix' atmospheric carbon dioxide and exhale life-giving oxygen. So long live the eco-warriors of The Philippines Bureau of Immigration and every other paper-consuming bureaucratic organisation!! Environmental heroes all!

* * *

Nine

We spent the first half of February worrying about getting our shipment. We were now in regular email contact with Asian Tigers of Taguig and we knew from them that the ship would be docking in Manila on Monday February 2nd. But we found, to our dismay, that there might be a problem. So far, the entire process of packing up in England and moving one's stuff eight thousand miles had been relatively straightforward. To ship one's entire household possessions across the world is not so difficult after all. It falls into the lowest class of life's problems, those which are easily solved by the simple tactic of moving money from one place to another place.

All our worldly possessions had duly disappeared in a van, to be re-crated and put into a 20 foot container for subsequent shipping via container ship to Manila via Singapore. I did find out from Monkey Removals that the journey time would be about a month and the shipment would be departing Southampton on December 29th, which meant that arrival in Manila would probably be at about the end of January.

It soon became clear from the non-replies to our emails that Monkey Removals were just one stage of a three-stage process and details of the second and third stages was not knowledge they were in possession of. They were unable to tell us the name of the company who would be handling the Philippines' end of the deal nor the name of the ship which would be carrying our container. I have since worked out how it all works but for several weeks between the end of November and receiving our first email contact with Asian Tigers of Manila at the end of January, we had no idea where our belongings were and when we would see them again.

What I think happens in the shipping industry is that the local shipper (I think they call themselves 'logistics specialists', these days.), in our case, Monkey Removals of Lincoln, would pack and crate all our belongings in

Father Toter Resuello led the blessing of the house at our housewarming party on March 17th. 2013

The famous ceremony of 'Throwing the Money'

a container and send it to the next stage where a broker at the docks, or container port, who will find a ship for it. When the ship docks at the other end, the shipping line will contact a local logistics specialist via a broker, who then liaises with the legal eventual recipient of the goods and who arranges customs clearance and final delivery. At least that's how I think it works. If that is indeed the way that it works, then it would explain the next little bit of nervousness we had to endure. If the three parts of the system work independently, then payment must be passed on from one part of it to the next. So the initial packer must pay the shipping line, after which the shipping line will need to pay the final deliverer. A couple of days after we had first been contacted by Asian Tigers, we got word from them that the shipping line, Anglo-Pacific, had not been paid by Monkey Removals before they had stowed our goods. This was very worrying because, according to Asian Tigers, there would be two expensive consequences. The first is that the goods could not be moved out of the Manila Container Terminal until all the payments had been made and storage on the dockside would incur daily taxes and 'demurrage' fees. The second possibility would be that we would need to put up an expensive bond to cover the cost of returning our shipment to the UK.

After the fateful news that Monkey Removals had not yet settled their bill with Anglo-Pacific, we made a series of anguished emails to them, imploring them to pay up so that we would be able to get our lives back again. The ship had docked on February 2nd and although the first five days of dockside storage are free, from the 7th of February the meter had been running. On February 12th, when we made our second trip to Taguig to get my passport back from Asian Tigers, now that the customs people no longer needed it, we tried to arrange a final delivery date. This time we took a jeepney from Base View Homes to the Lipa bus station, feeling that that would be safer than when we had made the same journey two weeks previously. I got my passport back and passed on the news that we still had not heard from Monkey Removals regarding the payment to the shipper. So, we paid P6000 on account for demurrage and taxes and we continued our frantic emails. I was afraid that the final costs for customs taxes and dock storage would come in at more than this, but I was pleasantly surprised when I eventually got a refund of P1934. On mature reflection, delaying payment makes perfectly good sense to the cost-conscious businessman, as Tim of Monkey Removals undoubtedly is. The extra costs of the delay in port charges and additional taxes are thrown on to the client, while the original contractor has use of client money for a little longer. He knows that there will be delays at final destination and can schedule his payments accordingly. It makes no sense at all to pay out a single centavo one minute before absolutely necessary. And what does it matter if the client is not kept informed and if he worries unduly? Clients always worry.

Finally, news came through on February 15th that the outstanding bill had been settled and as soon as Asian Tigers had confirmed that the Bureau of Customs had made their inspections and we had been cleared, our household goods were finally delivered on February 19th. There was little breakage from the long sea voyage, just the glass in a few pictures, easily replaced by a local glass cutter near Base View Homes Subdivision. The army of men from Asian Tigers arrived early in the morning, having left Manila as early as 4.30am. They competently and efficiently unloaded, assembled furniture and checked contents and were away before lunch.

Meanwhile, we were completing the development of our new house on several fronts simultaneously. Loydz prefers to avoid cooking smells in the house by cooking outside. This is the concept of what Filipinos call a 'dirty kitchen' – the house is kept clean-smelling and fresh because cooking is done in an outside service area. However, I was a little nervous about the cooker and washing machine being open to the elements and so we had the area covered in using a local carpenter. I also had a shed built for all my tools and various unused household artefacts. Finally, Loydz contacted a landscape gardener, Myla, who completely transformed the building site around the house into the beginnings of what we hope will, one day, become a lush tropical garden, full of brilliant colours and heady exotic scents. That, at least, is the dream.

We also got a TV system linked into CCTV for domestic security. It was also time to regularise our arrangements for electricity and water. With Cosette's help we went to the local electricity and water 'boards' to sign up for utilities supply.

While the house was still unfinished, we had relied for water and electricity on sharing supplies from another of the builder's projects, while the bills would be paid by Vic himself. But now was the time to pay up and go legal. Pretty soon, electrical and water engineers arrived to install meters, so we are now paying for our own supplies.

We also installed Venetian blinds in the main high-ceilinged sitting room. Loydz, who was responsible for the design, favours a very high room, in effect two storeys, the upper space where a third bedroom might have been. It is very impressive and the effect is startling. At first we were going to put Venetian blinds in the upper half of the room only, but they looked so good that we decided to put them in the lower half as well.

The house must be looking good to others because Engineer Vic and his brother often bring new potential clients to see it. From groundbreaking to its present finished state, there has been a stream of people to view Vic's handiwork. Typically they are an older European or American or Australian and his younger Filipina wife. Not too different from us, really.

Vic's brother is also a good businessman. One Friday evening, he turned up at our house with news of a new 24-hour massage service to be offered by one of our neighbours. Thank you, I politely told him, just leave your flyer. I was about to turn and go back in when he told me to meet the masseuses, a group of eight or so young Filipinas, none of whom looked older than about twenty, who got out of the car and stood pouting for my approval. I don't know if it was related incident, but a few days later, my wife received, on her cellphone, a call from a young woman who asked her 'you want sex?'

Loydz also hired a home help from the local community, a nice obliging Filipina called Leni. Leni is short for Elena, which of course, follows the standard naming convention. Home helps are always called

Helen or Helena, or at least mine always have been, just as every electrician I have ever employed has been called Dave.

We have CCTV for security although how effective it is, we cannot tell since we have never had cause to refer to it. This is a gated, secure community. The neatly-uniformed guards on the gates are armed and they are very strict about whom they admit. Only cars with a valid sticker are allowed in unchallenged - any driver entering the subdivision on legitimate business, such as a delivery, must leave a valid ID at the guardhouse. The guards quickly get to know the residents, whom they invariably greet with a smart military salute. Several times, people in our employ, Leni and others, have been stopped from visiting us for not having proper identification. We have had to phone through as well as provide written permission for them to enter the subdivision on our cognisance.

Many of the residents rely on dogs for their safety and security. This is, after all, a society with a violent streak and Base View Homes is definitely affluent, rich even, by local standards. As there is everywhere, there will be a criminal element attracted by the seeming wealth of the subdivision. Many dogs run loose and there are periodic clamp downs when owners are reminded to keep their dogs in or face the costs of retrieving them from the municipal dog pound after a mass round-up. Some dogs are kept in small cages, which would be regarded as cruel in countries like the dog-worshipping UK where the rights of animals are defended by strong laws backed up by draconian punishments. But here in The Philippines, no such sentimentality exists. Dogs are working animals whose job it is to warn of intruders. Unfortunately, they do their jobs only too well. Small packs of dogs run wild at night, keeping up continuous barking and yelping, making sleep unsettled. They greet every event – cars, motorcycles or pedestrians with a chorus of loud yelping, growling or barking. One can even hear dogs in the far distance responding in sympathy as one of the caged animals nearby starts up. It is one feature of life in this subdivision which is certainly not to our liking.

By the end of February, about seven months after we had started on this adventure, we had a comfortable house. Our garden was planted, the painting was finished, we were connected up to all those indispensable services of modern civilisation such as water, electricity, telephone and the Internet. I had a shed and a comfortable office. We had, effectively, moved our entire English house and our English lives, lock, stock and barrel to Lipa, in The Philippines. All the bills had been paid, the works had all been completed to our satisfaction, the house was looking good and we were ready to settle into a routine. I was even starting to lose my fear of driving our big car on the local roads. There will still be things to do of course, but we had completed much of what we had set out to achieve.

All that remained was the blessing and house-warming, scheduled for March 17th, the Sunday following Loydz' birthday, when a fair proportion of her numerous friends and family could be present.

About 80 of them showed up. Actually, the guest numbers at any Filipino affair are always variable. It is considered quite acceptable to gatecrash, if you have some connection, however tenuous, with the host. So, in addition to Loydz' family, and her sometime office colleagues, there were people from the subdivision offices and the builder's family to make up the numbers. We had employed caterers, a local firm led by an enterprising young businessman called Auster, who owns several hospitality facilities in Lipa including a hotel/events center, and a restaurant cum nightclub. Lots of the guests also brought extra food with the result that we had enough to feed a small city. It is usual in The Philippines, when going to a party to take food, always something special, just as in England one might take a bottle of wine. Accordingly, our guests brought us *siomai*, (small savory dumplings), pork barbecue, rice cakes, birthday cakes and chocolate plus a very Filipino favorite, green mangoes and shrimp paste. I had also over-bought on wine and beer so we could accommodate the traditional expected extras of 20% or so above the numbers who had actually been formally invited.

We took the opportunity to employ the services of a young priest from the local seminary to do a house blessing. He did a very nice two-for-one offer by blessing the car as well. As one who lapsed his Catholicism in

1947, the blessing of inanimate objects is strange for me, especially especially sprinkling them with holy water from a little plastic bottle. But, hell, who knows, it can't do any harm and, you never know, it might just make me feel a little safer when I venture out into the warzone in our people-carrier!

After the blessing of all the rooms and the counterpoint of invocations and responses, there was the ceremony of 'throwing the money'. What this entailed was that Loydz and I climbed up the staircase carrying plates of the peso coins we had been saving over the previous few weeks. At a signal from the priest, we threw them down for the children to collect in a mad scramble. It is supposed to be lucky and it probably is, at least for those children who escaped being hit in the bombardment and came out with a miniscule profit.

Everything gets blessed in this country. Had we not been hung over on the Monday following our party, we had an invitation from the organizers of the subdivision that we could attend the formal blessing of the water storage tower which had been newly refurbished.

Filipino celebrations follow a standard pattern. First there is the huge amount of food accompanied by iced water or lemonade. When everyone is full, the drinking starts for the drinkers. The non-drinkers tend to leave earlier as the party rowdies up. When everyone is well lubricated, all are obliged to do a turn on the video karaoke. The songs I always sing are *Autumn Leaves, As Time Goes By* and *Summertime*. All nice and slow and easy to sing. Songs, in fact, for those of us who still hold to the view that real music ended with the Beatles first LP.

I think everyone had a good time. Philippines parties are not unlike those in the UK, or, I suppose anywhere else where having a good time is important. The big difference in The Philippines is that the musical part of the evening means singing to the karaoke machine instead of dancing to a disco. Both forms of musical treat are equally embarrassing for us old farts. Seeing or hearing some of us dance or sing makes for perfect blackmail material either way.

So, how will it play out, this latest stage of a long and varied life? Well, I obviously hope. This country is naturally beautiful. Its rulers have sensibly resisted imported industrialization, so there is no Toyota factory in an industrial estate on the edge of town. The multinationals are here, but not in strength. Starbucks and the ubiquitous McDonalds ply their trades and there are one or two developers of shopping complexes and tower blocks. But the tower blocks are mainly confined to one or two areas in Manila. Here in Lipa, it still feels like the 1950's. The businesses are mainly small independent stores and shops. There is a lot to be said for economic underdevelopment. It means that The Philippines still retains much of its charm and simplicity. There is little serious crime except maybe at election time, when some politicians hire hit men to erase each other. But that is an occupational hazard in many countries. There is reported high-level graft and corruption, of course, but show me a country where there isn't. All in all, The Philippines remains something of a backwater and, should the world economy continue its present downwards course, it may never attract the loose big international building-investment money which has been the ruin of so many of the world's former beautiful places like the Mediterranean.

Loydz is now happily into gardening and domesticity. I do my writing. Sometimes I get nostalgic for my old life as an itinerant teacher on the road from city to city or country to country but that was then and this is now. That part of my life is over. I have even stored away my diplomas and academic regalia. I can't see any future occasion when I will need to dig them out. I have not been addressed as 'Doctor' or 'Professor' for nearly two years now. I even have a book for teaching oneself Basic Tagalog.

Life here in Lipa is permanent summertime. The living is easy. A nice house, a pretty wife, everything taken care of. Low cost of living, domestic help to take care of the chores. The sun shines most days now that the wet season is over and we are moving into a tropical summer. I get a few insect bites which are mildly irritating but it seems that my

Filipino friends don't get them. So I am assuming that I too, in time, will develop the same immunity.

There is a traditional weekly power cut. Occasionally, it will last all day but mostly the outages are only minutes long. During a long brown-out, it means that we can't use the Internet. That is actually a blessing in disguise because it means that I can read some of the large number of books I had been promising myself. Anyway, power cuts are part of the stuff of life. I have read that they will even become a standard feature of living in England when the British shut down half of their power stations in about two years time.

∗ ∗ ∗

Postscript

Since I wrote this memoir of emigration to the Philippines, I have had more time to adjust to and to reflect upon, my new situation. I have now enjoyed eight months as a *Lipeño* and I am starting to see the cultural differences and similarities between Europe and the Philippines from a longer perspective.

Some cultural differences are immense. For example, to a European, the strength of organised Christianity is like something from history. Most of us Europeans don't do religion anymore. Hundreds of years of religious conflict have turned us all into atheists of one sort or another. European Christianity clings on here and there, but if we think about Christianity at all, it is part of a historical framework which has contributed much to our heritage but is now in terminal decline. We see Christianity as part of the European cultural, or more likely tourist, background. There are cathedrals for the tourists and charming ceremonies at Christmas and Easter which, are, as often as not, religion-free and which, these days, resemble more and more the pre-Christian pagan marking of the seasons, rather than celebrations of biblical events. Officially, the British do have an established religion, the Church of England, but Anglicanism, with its relaxed demotic rituals and its regular navel-gazing over issues like gay marriage or women bishops, remains just this side of being quaintly ridiculous. It is something which is only wheeled out at national events like a royal wedding.

Not so in the Philippines. Here Roman Catholicism is fervently, devoutly practised by the majority of the population. Perhaps it is because the country has never had to suffer the sort of religious wars which have been a recurrent feature of European culture in the last thousand years from the Crusades to Northern Ireland, that the established Catholic Church here has never had to face any opposition. As a result, its influence extends right throughout Philippine society. On Sundays, the churches run a continuous schedule of masses - no respectable Filipino will miss the Sunday service. The two large shopping malls in Lipa both hold hour-long church services in their central atriums. These melanges of God and Mammon are attended by hundreds of people. There will be maybe five hundred chairs laid out in the cruciform aisles of the mall with a large dais in one of the arms of the cross where the priests perform their celebrations. The congregation must arrive early to get a seat. Many are disappointed and scores of worshippers have to stand behind the chairs or outside in the hot sun, faces pressed against the glass windows. At the end of the hour's communal worship, the chairs and the dais with the altar are hurriedly cleared away so that regular trading can begin.

Religious devotions continue throughout the week. Even on weekdays the local churches do a roaring trade. On Wednesday afternoons particularly, they host regular capacity crowds. Religious iconography is everywhere and most homes will give over a little space to a carefully-tended makeshift altar on which will be placed crucifixes and statuettes of saints. Philippine good manners requires that no meal can be begun without the diners first crossing themselves. Many offices suspend operations for a short time once or twice a day for in order that the workers can say prayers.

This loyalty to conventional religion does have some far-reaching social consequences. The Catholic Church continues to have a lot of influence in government, some of it reactionary to Western eyes. For example, there is still no divorce in the Philippines. Marriages can be ended but only by annulment and that requires collusion between the separating partners and with their external advisers such as psychiatrists and legal counsel. Abortion is still a non-issue and even contraception, while obviously practiced because middle-class women do not have more than 2.4 children, is still a taboo subject. On the other hand, homosexuality, which remains a sensitive subject in the West, is openly tolerated. There is even, some afternoons, a top-rated afternoon TV beauty contest for transsexuals, or 'ladyboys'. In this regard the Philippines appears more progressive than the West. For example, the performers in a night club chorus line are selected without gender discrimination - the girls and the ladyboys are indistinguishable to the audience.

I still have to come to terms with driving on the local roads. There are no rules, save the ineffectual hand-waving of the odd policeman which no-one takes any notice of. The roads are painted with white lines but lane discipline is not a Philippine concept. Drivers will cut in on both sides and pedestrians will amble slowly between the moving cars without even turning to look in the direction of the approaching vehicles. Motorised tricycles and jeepneys, the two forms of short-distance Lipa public transport, will aggressively charge across the traffic stream, defying the oncoming drivers to stop and let them through, which they always do. The only rule, as far as I can see, is that if a road-user, be they pedestrian or juggernaut, sees a few feet of empty road ahead, then they move into it. Somehow it all gets sorted out.

I have deferred getting a Philippine driver's licence partly out of fear of using the roads and partly because my capable wife will drive me on those rare occasions when we need to use the car, such as the twice-monthly trip to the supermarket. She understands the Philippine driving style and I do not. Her complaint about me is that I am too well-mannered on the road, that I am too happy to stop and give way to other drivers when the local style would be to blow the horn loudly to warn the others to give one a wide berth. Consequently, I confine my driving to taking her to the subdivision gates when she needs to go into town by jeepney. I am also called upon occasionally to manoeuvre our large people-carrier in and out of tight parking spots, something which I can do without feeling, as I certainly would if I drove on the busy roads, the imminent onset of a nervous breakdown. I think the cultural difference between driving in Europe and driving in the Philippines can be summed up by the use of the horn and the flash of headlights. In Europe, the horn is only used sparingly, as a gentle alert. Flashing one's headlights means, in Europe, 'after you, Claude'. Here the horn is used more loudly. It is also a warning but one with much more aggressive significance - 'if you want to live, get out of my way!'. The flashing of headlights has the opposite meaning to the English one. Here it means simply – 'You wait! Me first!'

As an expatriate, I have to go to Manila frequently. When we go, we leave the car behind and get the bus. The distance is only about 70 kilometres but the bus can take from one to three hours depending on the time of day and the traffic density at the Manila end. But the journey only costs about P100 pp each way and the buses are air-conditioned and comfortable. In Manila we get around by taxi. I am probably letting the side down a little by using public transport since the preferred vehicle for well-to-do Filipinos is the black or silver heavy 4x4 with tinted windows. My neighbours wash them religiously in all weathers. But I can plead my age and my English eccentricity to explain my antisocial position when it comes to not conforming to the automotive stereotype.

Another feature of local life is the way everyone seems to be in some small business or other. The whole economy is based upon small businesses in a way that England has not seen for forty or fifty years. I can well remember my home town in the 1950's. All the streets and the main roads were lined by small one-man or family concerns. That was before the High Streets were taken over for the exclusive use of the well-known large retail chains. When I was young, there were a few national chains, like Woolworths and some others now long forgotten, but on the whole, commerce in Oldham in the 1950's was about little businesses which could afford to trade from advantageous locations. That culture no longer exists in the West where business is the province of the multinationals or the big brand names. A small northern English town could then support, maybe four or five bookshops. Now there is only Waterstones and WH Smith, with, maybe, the odd small independent, clinging on in defiance of the laws of business economics.

Here in Lipa, small businesses thrive. For example, there is a small part of the town centre given over to numerous independent pharmacies who continue to trade even in the presence of Mercury Drug, the largest Philippine pharmacy chain. How many British towns and cities have to rely solely on Boots for their pharmaceutical services? In the West, the elimination of business bio-diversity in favour of the big conglomerates may well be the Philippine future as well. But I hope not. It is encouraging to see the survival of the endangered species, the small independent firm. It is basic capitalism at its best.

There are international trade names here, of course. McDonalds, Starbucks, Kentucky Fried Chicken and a few others have all staked their claims in most towns. But, for the most part, business life here is home-grown. In spite of that, many things one might think would be difficult to obtain are fully available. There are not many things which I might need which I cannot get hold of as easily, and often more cheaply, than I could in the UK.

Another related feature of Philippine life is the way people seem to have little private enterprises to bring in a little extra cash. In my youth, people would set up small shops in their front rooms to earn a little money in a cash-poor society. Here in Lipa, the same thing goes on. Some houses have small front-room businesses attached – they might sell purified drinking water or bread. They are like mini-convenience stores.

Many women, usually women – this is a matriarchy- sell small items from mail-order catalogues or grow vegetables for sale. Others might offer home-manicures or hair-cutting. The rewards will be small but they are a vital lifeline in a low-wage economy. Their menfolk will often be OFW's, Overseas Filipino Workers, or low-paid artisans. The versatility of the Filipino manual worker can often impress – a bricklayer may easily turn into an electrician or a car mechanic should the right job turn up. Manual workers, those in the building trade especially, usually do not have permanent contracted employment. Instead they must present themselves for work each morning and hope that there will be a day's work for them. This employment system is also redolent of England before the 1970's when 'the lump', as it was then known, was abolished by law.

Medical care here in the Philippines is first-class if you can afford to pay for it. I have not yet been hospitalised, but the care I have received since my arrival has been of a standard higher than that I received in the UK under the National Health Service. The doctors I have met are excellent. Most are US-trained and they treat the patients as grown-ups, quite unlike the patronising British general practitioner. Here I am entrusted with my own medical records and X-rays and my various conditions and the treatments for them are explained to me with precision and respect. How sensible this is, instead of relying on a vast hidden repository of paper records for every NHS patient which are kept confidential even from the patients themselves? (Details of costs of medications etc. are given in appendix B.)

One feature of Philippine society which everyone is agreed upon is the labyrinthine bureaucracy, which exists, as far as one can tell, merely to provide employment and economic activity. It is, I suppose, no worse than Western bureaucracies in its complexity and I certainly prefer to work with the Philippines Bureau of Immigration than the United Kingdom Border Agency, if only for the superior friendliness and humanity of the Philippine service. The differences lie in the attitudes, the costs and the level of personal service of the two comparable organisations. On the whole, though, it seems to me that the quantities of paper-shuffling and form-filling are pretty much the same the world over, in every country.

Apart from immigration, which has been a running sore of a problem for both Loydz and myself in whatever country we have found ourselves, setting up a business here is not simple thing. Most small one-man businesses are just set up. This is certainly what you would do if you wanted to sell your garden plants or home-grown vegetables. One day you don't have a business, the next day you do. That's about it. Unfortunately the kind of business I had in mind required a necessary interaction with Philippine officialdom. Otherwise I would not have got involved.

The business I now have, after my struggle against the bureaucrats, is a small publishing house for start-up authors who want to self-publish, like me and anyone else who wants to have a go at becoming the next Dan Brown. To do it properly, one needs to get ISBN numbers for each of the company's publications. The ISBN or International Standard Book Number is a unique identifier for each of the world's billions of books.

Here in the Philippines, the issuing of new ISBN's is a monopoly of the National Library of the Philippines in Manila

Unfortunately, one can't just go to the National Library, fill up a form, pay the money and get an ISBN for your book just like that. Oh no, one must first have a business name and a business permit. Business names are registered with the Department of Trade and Industry in Lipa City, and cost P2015. But that was just step one on the long road to getting a business permit. A business permit was only granted to me after two days of visits to the town hall, the local municipal office for our home district or *barangay*, plus the obtaining of certificates of permission from the subdivision.

Each stage in this two-week long process involved the exchange of money and sometimes the filling of yet more forms. Actually, we didn't need to fill up a form at every stage - some stages only involved the exchange of money. Even though I will be a one-man business sitting in front of my computer in my house just like I was doing before Lipa Publishing was formed, I still needed the permission of the sanitation, garbage, planning and engineering departments of the municipality , not to say the mayor's office (A fee of P250, added on for good luck, I guess.)

The business permit itself comes with a metal plaque which looks like a car number plate. Printed on it are my special number and a picture of the mayor. I am now in business! Well, only for the next four months, until the end of the year. Then I have to make a new application and go through the whole two-week process once again.

Another impediment to business efficiency is the postal system. Letters take about three weeks to get back and forth to Europe by surface mail. Airmail is available, but it is expensive. I was quoted P1050 (about £15) to send an ordinary letter back to the UK by air. Local mail services work, after a fashion but there is no scheduled letter-box collection and daily delivery as we have in Europe. One must post letters at the Post Office in the centre of Lipa or in the SM shopping mall. For really important items and certainly for sending anything valuable, one must use a commercial courier like DHL which is well-established here in the Philippines.

But local Internet services are very good and if one wants to start a small online business from here, it is quite possible. Lipa Publishing will be operating almost entirely online and I think I can make it work, using contacts in other parts of the world. Anyone reading this who would like to do something similar is very welcome to email me at *lipapub@yahoo.com.ph* and I will be glad to help.

If you are into eating, then the Philippines is definitely for you. Meals are taken at regular mealtimes and a programme of breakfast, mid-morning snacks, lunch, mid-afternoon snacks, dinner, evening snacks is the invariable pattern of Philippine eating. Most meals include rice and the Philippine preferred taste tends to savoury dishes well-salted. This takes some adjustment since the diet is quite different than that which I am used to in England. My wife is a good adaptable cook and there are many European, Japanese and Chinese restaurants. In fact, it is difficult to move very far in a Philippine city without coming upon a restaurant. It is almost as if the entire country is constantly eating.

An interesting feature of Philippine entertaining is that even if the hostess has provided a sumptuous spread for the expected number of guests plus the traditional 20% or so of expected 'walk-ins', the guests will also bring plenty of extra food. Some guests will even take over the kitchen and cook food themselves. It is normal, at the end of a Philippine party, for all the guests to take home the surplus food in 'doggy' bags.

The climate still requires constant adjustment for a European from a cold, wet country. The summer peak can reach 35C for days on end. Even the night-time temperature will not fall much below 26C during that time of the year, which lasts roughly from April to July. Fans and air-conditioning are in continuous use round the clock.

As I write this, at the end of August, we are in the middle of the wet season. At first the rains appear once a day for a few minutes only, like late April showers. But as the season builds up, the rains get longer and heavier until this times of the year we are in the middle of a succession of typhoons and tropical storms which follow in an almost unbroken sequence, with maybe no more than a couple of days respite before a violent storm and its successor. This year, 2013, has seen even worse flooding than usual. In one week of storms, the rainfall in Manila exceeded twice the long-term monthly average. When moving to the Philippines it is a good idea to research your intended location carefully to make sure it is not in a region where flooding is likely. Our house is on the crest of a gentle slope and has been well weatherproofed. We have been able to listen to the downpours, which can last all day or longer, in dry comfort although their noise is often loud enough to drown out the sound of the TV.

Earlier in the year, we had a series of daily power cuts which were advertised in advance. The local electricity provider, Batelec, (for Batangas Electricity Board) was doing engineering work. With advance knowledge of an outage we would use the opportunity to visit Manila or spend the day at one of Lipa's two large shopping malls and do our shopping. Lately, the advertised blackouts have ceased but we still get the occasional break in electrical service. Sometimes the power cuts last a few minutes or even a few seconds, sometimes, very occasionally, a few hours. I cannot complain that they are particularly inconvenient. We light candles or use a flashlight or lamps and we wait for the power to return. Lamps with rechargeable batteries sell well – electricity here is not expensive. (appendix B) Maybe this acceptance is evidence that I am slowly acclimatising to my new life as a Lipeño?

When I first came here eight months ago, our house was one of the outermost of the houses which make up the Base View Homes Subdivision. But since then there has been a steady stream of new building projects. Only a few months ago, I could look out from my kitchen window across an almost unbroken jungle of grass and trees. At night, there were no house- or street lights. But now, just this short time later, several new houses have sprung up. There is a mini-building boom going on. Soon, I am sure, we will find our precious isolation will have given way to new neighbours. We have discovered that the building lots are selling quickly and we have purchased a small lot adjacent to our house so that we will not be enclosed on all sides if the overgrown field behind us is ever completely built. Hopefully, that will not happen for a while yet and we can continue to enjoy the feeling of living in a semi-rural location.

The incessant chorus of dogs' barking is still a feature of our nights but we are now used to it and we now sleep through the non-stop point and counterpoint of howls and yelps. The Philippine attitude to dogs is that they are working animals, there to give the alarm should there be an intruder. They would not be able, if there were an intruder, to do much more than sound the alarm because often they are penned up twenty-four hours a day in small constricting cages. How effective their alarms would be is also doubtful, given that there is always, at any time, at least one dog, somewhere nearby, in the subdivision, loudly making its presence known. The caging of these animals in 'cells of little ease', where they can hardly turn around, would bring prosecutions for animal cruelty in the UK, where dogs are regularly treated like one of the family. The English, it has been noted, will often lavish more affection on their dogs than they would on their children. Personally, I am neutral on dogs. I don't like them enough to want to have one in my house, as many English do. On the other hand I am a little uneasy at the casual cruelty of imprisoning a dog in a cage where it can hardly move.

So, how do I like being an expat in the Philippines? It is a good place to live. The people are charming, with a kind of innocence, long gone from people in the cynical West. Lipa is a safe place to live and all the services one might need are to hand. Many parts of English culture – the football, the pubs, the London cultural scene, English food – were not things I was involved in. I can take or leave football and pubs. I rarely went to London, although when I did, I enjoyed it. As for English food, these days that seems to mean kebabs, burgers, pizza and curry which are available everywhere.

* * *

Appendix A - what it all cost us.

Anyone contemplating emigration should be sure to keep a tight rein on their finances. One finds that demands on one's pocket come thick and fast and it is easy to lose track of payments when one is signing several cheques a day. I recommend a good spreadsheet and disciplined systematic recording of every outgoing. That is what I did. I can't put hand on heart and swear that I kept track of everything but the following balance sheet is not too far off reality. It's in the right ball park, as they say.

	Pesos
Building costs in Philippines	
Cost of lot	1,080,000
(240 sqm lot at P5000 /sqm less 10% cash discount)	
Building costs	
Tranche 1	1,000,000
Tranche 2	1,000,000
Tranche 3	1,000,000
Final payment at sign-off	200,000
Total costs of building and land	**4,280,000**

Extra costs for house completion etc.

	Pesos
CCTV	35,000
Appliances –air con./TVetc	90,760
Water and electricity connection	10,005
Shed, cover of service area, etc.	65,891
Internal – soft furnishings	91,658
Furniture	52,138
Internet/TV installation	11,440
Car, s/h Suzuki APV inc. registration	265,000
Garden landscaping	45,000
House-warming	44,000
Total extra costs for completion	**710,892**

Administrative etc. costs

	Pesos	Sterling
One year 13-A immigration visa	12,000	
Shipping costs	4,064	£4,035
Air fares		£1,231
Short term interest costs		£350
Rent of temporary apartment(1 mon.)	12,500	
Total administrative costs	**28,564**	
Total peso costs	**5,019,456**	
Total sterling costs		**£5,616**
Overall total project cost	**5,388,480**	**£86,730**

For the purpose of this exercise, I used a notional average exchange rate for the period August 2012 to March 2013 of 62 pesos to the pound sterling.

Appendix B - what it costs to live in The Philippines

The cost of living in any country where there is a big resident expatriate community is the source of a million web pages and blogs. Much of the published information is what I would call 'back-packer' friendly i.e. for the young and footloose. This memoir is aimed at an older generation, with different tastes, so while there exist many descriptions on how to live cheaply in The Philippines – just google 'Cost of living in The Philippines' and a hundred websites will arise before you – I can only give my first-hand experience of what it costs to live a settled retired life here. I don't know, for example, what it costs to go to a Manila nightclub but if that is what you want to know, there are a million bloggers out there ready to tell you.

As always, the biggest expense is accommodation. We have a little experience of renting in this country when we stayed in a small apartment in Manila which was quite close to the city centre. We got it at a discounted rent because the owner is a cousin of my wife. But we understand that his commercial rate for renting a one-bedroom basic condominium in central Manila would be about P25,000 per month.

Food is cheap. We spend approximately P15,000 per month at the supermarket. We are not big eaters and we find we can obtain many of the same foods as we would in Europe. The following is a typical list of costs.

Chicken	- up to P150/kg;
Bread	– P38-60 for a loaf.
Pandesal, small sweet bread rolls, cost about P2-3 each;	
Pork	– maybe P170-190 per kilo depending on the cut;
Orange juice	– pure orange juice, imported, costs about P90/litre;
Eggs	– P4-5 each;
Bananas	– P50-60/kg;

Grapes	– P200-240/kg;
Butter	– P120/250gm;
Milk	– P75/litre;
Cheese	– P400/kg;

These prices are inclusive of 12% VAT.

Fish can be expensive but is generally of good quality. Bangus, the local favourite costs about P120-150/kg; tilapia is P100-120/kg;

Rice, the staple of all Filipino meals, comes in various types and costs from P35-50/k

Drinking water is bought in large 15 litre containers costing about P35 each. There is an initial deposit of P200 and two of us consume one full container per week.

Alcohol – the local beer is a very light lager called San Miguel and costs about P33 a can. European or American beer costs about twice this. For wine, a decent bottle of Australian red will set you back about P350. Generally wine prices are a little lower than in the UK – from P300-600 (£5-£10) for *plonko rosso*. If you prefer cocktails, then a litre of local gin or vodka or brandy can be had for as little as P200.

Eating out is anything from a sidewalk cafe at P100 a head up to P2000 at the posher places. A good Japanese restaurant in Makati which we use, charges about P500 a head (or about £9) for a decent spread.

A coffee and burger at McDonalds will come to about P100-150.

Domestic costs are low. Electricity for a medium sized house using air conditioning during the hot season will average out at about P3000 a month. Metered tap water costs for two showering, washing clothes etc. comes in at about P400. This figure may be higher than usual because it includes a lot of water used when the garden was first planted and needed twice-daily watering.

A TV plan via satellite runs at about P900 monthly.

There are set up costs for Internet. These will be about P2500 initially with monthly costs of around P900 for the slowest package. If you want high-speed broadband to watch movies, for example, the costs go up steeply, maybe to P3000-4000 a month, depending on provider. It is possible to install a landline, and there are plans for optical fibre high-speed broadband even in provincial Lipa, but for the time being, here in Lipa, most people do not usually use landlines.

The cellphone is ubiquitous. One can buy 'load' for one's cellphone almost everywhere. There are three main providers, Globe, Sun Cellular and Smart Bro. Charges for calls between phones on the same network are free but phoning outside the network can be expensive. A 5-minute international call to the UK costs about P150.

There are also pay-as-you-go cards for Internet connections. We used them before our domestic wireless router had been installed. They are a little unreliable and they are certainly expensive if you use the Internet a lot – about P100 for an hour or so.

Big-ticket white goods and electronics are mainly imported from Japan and Korea and consequently you will pay about the same in The Philippines as you would in the US or Europe. The same applies to cars.

For us there are also fees for the costs of living in a gated community – to pay for the guards, cut the grass and collect the trash etc. The charge for these services has recently been raised from P400 to P550 per month per household.

Labour is cheap, so one can get hard-working home help for as little as P300 a day. Costs of gardeners, carpenters, plasterers and so on are only a fraction of the British or American equivalent prices. It is not worth trying to 'do it yourself' as we would in England where labour is expensive. Here, if you want a job done, there is someone ready to do it at a very affordable price. A plasterer or tiler or carpenter, may earn P500 a day. It is all 'cash in hand'.

Travelling around the city or the country is also cheap. Gasoline, at about P54 a litre, costs much less than you would pay in Europe. – diesel is about P44/litre. For a special trip, one could use a driver, either to drive his car at maybe P1500 daily, or, if he is driving your car, you might expect to pay P500-700 a day for his services. For very short journeys in towns, there are motorised or pedal-driven tricycles. A ride in one of these will only cost P20. A ride in a jeepney, here in Lipa, costs only P8. There are no taxis in Lipa but in Manila a taxi ride of say, three kilometres, may cost no more than P120. The motorised tricycle is the Lipeño equivalent of a taxicab and costs about P80 a kilometre.

Other services such as a haircut, can vary in price. A decent man's haircut at a salon in the shopping mall, may cost up to P200. A woman's cut, styling and colouring costs between P800 and P2500 depending on the salon.

A night in a mid-range hotel will cost about P3000 in Manila and between P1000 and P2500 in the provinces.

Medical costs are a permanent problem for the over-70's. In the UK, all of the costs would be met by the National Health Service. In The Philippines all medical costs must be met personally unless one has medical insurance, which is not available for someone of my age. Daily medication, essential and optional, cost me approximately P150 a day. In addition I need a monthly bottle of eye drops to treat my glaucoma. This costs about P1300.

My monthly outlay for routine medications therefore costs me about P5800, or approximately £85. A session of treatment at Manila's excellent Asian Eye Hospital costs about P15000 and that should be repeated every three months.

A consultation with a top local doctor costs about P500. A small emergency at A&E in Lipa's top private hospital, set me back about P13,000 which included a CT scan costing P8000.

My medical costs, total annually, therefore, about P100,000 or approximately P8500 monthly (plus emergencies, of course) or about £130 per month. (Say, $200) Maybe I am exceptional, although I don't think so. One of the reasons why people can enjoy increased longevity and a better quality of life in old age is because of modern pharmaceuticals. It is money well-spent.

As for supplies of these medications, there are several pharmacies in Lipa where branded or generic drugs can be bought over the counter. Many of the drugs which are strictly controlled by prescription in the UK are freely available here. Only the more serious medications require a doctor's prescription.

Fortunately, medical costs and food items attract a 20% discount and relief of the 12% VAT for holders of the Senior Citizen's Card. The card will also attract discounts to transport and other services and is a very useful possession for the Filipino retiree. The Philippine government generously extends its benefits to those of its expatriate guests who have permanent residency.

One of the good things about Philippine medical provision is that the patient is permitted to take away copies of his records including laboratory tests and X-rays. The effect of this is that patients are made personally responsible for their own medical history. They are also responsible for arranging their own follow-up appointments. This seems to be a more adult way of doing things than that of the NHS in the UK, where a patient's records are only available to registered medical practitioners.

* * *

Appendix C - what you need to do in your home country before you emigrate.

This a checklist of some of the many things one needs to do on leaving one's home country and emigrating abroad. It is not comprehensive: everyone's personal list will be different. But this is what we did.

1. Draw up a timeline for moving. Do this as soon as your house is reasonably likely to be sold. Allow at least two weeks after handing over the keys to your old house before getting on the plane – there will be numerous odds and ends to tie up after the house sale has been completed. Give yourself plenty of time. Get a well-charged cellphone. Make sure you have somewhere to stay during this interim period.

2. Arrange bank facilities in your new country. Some banks have branches all over the world but others are more localised. If you are expecting to be remitting money regularly, the costs can mount up. Most banks (and Western Union) charge a flat fee for the transfer, usually about £25. But you must also add on to that the bank's commission. Nor will you get the published exchange rate. In most cases these extras will add up to a loss of 1-2% at each end of the transaction. There are commercial money-transfer companies who do these transactions online and claim to undercut the regular banks but I have not used them. A good idea is to reduce the number of transfers to the minimum – e.g. making one large transfer every few months rather than regular monthly remittances. Another option is to find a bank with branches in both countries which will do the transfers for minimal cost.

    Remember also that many countries, including The Philippines, have strict laws about money laundering and will not allow you to make bank deposits in local accounts until you have proved yourself by establishing long-term residency.

If you are going to be living off pension income, then make sure the various pension authorities know what you are doing. Personally, I have my pensions paid into a British HSBC Premier account so that, eventually, I should be able to make regular transfers of money to The Philippines at zero cost, although I am still subject to the vagaries of the exchange rate. I let the sums build up in the UK, so that I am making remittances only two or three times a year at times when I judge that the exchange rate will be most favourable.

3. Redirect your mail. The Philippine mail service is slow and unreliable. Mail arriving from the UK or the US often goes 'missing', as happened to us.

A safer option is to use a commercial courier like DHL or UPS. But these services are very expensive and should only be used for valuable items such as important documents. These days mail can be delivered anywhere but what I did before leaving the UK was to arrange for my mail to be redirected to my daughter's address in England so that she could collect all the important-looking mail and forward it as a monthly package. This is considerably cheaper and certainly more reliable than giving the Royal Mail our address in The Philippines. Once you have paid for mail direction, the service kicks in only after five days, so be sure to get your timing right or you may miss important correspondence at a critical time.

4. Cancel payments to the phone, water, electricity and gas companies. If you have been paying by direct debit, then they will almost certainly owe you money. They will be coy and reluctant about repaying you. One of their favourite tricks is to allow you only to cancel a contract online. The website for doing this will give you an electronic form to fill up. Very likely they will ignore your form and you will need to telephone them several times before they will send you a paper cheque even if they still have

access to your bank details. Sky, the broadcaster, provides a form but also requires you to telephone an office in Glasgow. The number appears in very small type at the foot of their 'Contact us' page. If you have a multipart contract, such as TV, landline, broadband altogether, then you will need to cancel each part separately. I am sure other digital media companies will do the same thing.

5. Cancel the Council Tax payments. These too, need to be done online, which you will need to follow up by phone calls, letters and, in my case, at Lincoln, a personal visit. Be prepared for the excuse 'the computer was down' when you ask why the form was ignored. That is what computers are for, to blame when human beings are found lacking.

6. Cancel house and car insurances. These too, will require the gradual building of a relationship with the company which owes you money as you are passed from office to office and telephone to telephone. This is why you cannot just up sticks and leave the country. If the various organisations you are dealing with know that you are going to emigrate then they will drag their heels even more.

7. If you take regular medication, you must get at least three months' worth in advance, more if possible, until you establish a source of supply in your new country. Keep a record of your repeat prescription for the doctor in your new country. Doctors do not like to share patient information, even with the patient himself, but, here and there, one can find a doctor who will even copy the notes for a patient. If you are tended by such a rare humanitarian, then take advantage of his/her generosity. Unfortunately, many doctors take the opposite view that their patients cannot be trusted with medical information about themselves.

8. Try to get a list of all things unobtainable in your new country. Such things as dried herbs and olive oil are rare luxuries in The

Philippines, so I stocked up on them during a special shopping trip to Tesco. Remember, of course, to buy them before the shippers arrive to pack up.

9. Sell your car in good time. The important thing is to get a decent price for it. If you mention that you are emigrating, the car's value will, mysteriously, plummet. Even if you still have a week or two to go, the price of renting a temporary vehicle may well be less than the loss you might take on a forced car sale. Beware of the 'false damage scam' which many car rental companies try on. You may have kept the rental car in perfect condition but if you are turning it in at an airport, the company will know that you are leaving the country and will discover, to everyone's amazement, that you have scratched it and the tiny scratch will, somehow, cost hundreds of pounds to repair which will be immediately deducted from your credit card. If you are aware of this scam, then you can avoid it by cancelling the card, which you may have to do anyway, as soon as you have rented the car and before you return it at the airport.

10. Send contact details to everyone else you have dealings with. In my case I informed a couple of learned societies of which I am a member and, naturally enough, my publishers.

11. Final packing is important. It is not worth packing anything which is worth less than what you can buy it for at your destination. It is a good idea to buy one of those small hand-held spring balances to check the weight of your luggage. It is easy to overestimate what you can take with you on the plane and excess baggage charges are huge. It makes no sense to pack an old pair of jeans weighing maybe a kilo when excess baggage is charged at £50 a kilo and a new pair of blue jeans in Manila will set you back no more than ten pounds.

12. When shipping appliances or white goods, be sure that they will work in the new country. British TV sets or DVD players do not work in The Philippines so unless you need your old TV to play

old VHS tapes, it is best to try to find it a new home in the UK. The same applied, much to our surprise, to our almost-new washing machine, which did not work in The Philippines because the local electricity has a mains frequency of 60Hz, unlike the 50Hz of the UK. The electrician was aware of the problem which, he explained, is due to the 'windings' on the motor. The motor needed replacing, or a new, Filipino-specific washing machine would need to be bought.

Then it is just a matter of going round to say one's goodbyes, enjoy the farewell parties and try not to be too hung over when you get the early morning flight.

***

Appendix D - what are the customs requirements for The Philippines?

The Philippines customs regulations are not too different from elsewhere. Obviously one cannot bring into the country obvious items like weapons or drugs. On the whole, the customs rules make perfect common sense.

The customs declaration you make on the plane before landing asks if you are bringing any jewellery into the country, I answered no to this because I did not want to explain that I had felt it safer to bring my watches and my wife's personal jewellery with me on the plane, rather than risk putting it in storage or in the check-in suitcase. However, its value was not inconsiderable but I reckoned that the prohibition on importing jewellery is mainly directed against serious traders in precious stones and metals and against money-launderers. I interpreted the restriction to mean that one's personal effects, which one did not intend to sell, would be exempt, although the small customs form does not make that clear. One cannot bring into The Philippines large amounts of cash. All personal holdings of more than $10,000 (USD) must be declared at port of entry.

The customs officers are very suspicious of multiples of the same item. One ex-customs official who came to do some work on our house did mention that anyone trying to bring in, as in the case he mentioned, five laptop computers, would certainly find them confiscated. The same applies to large numbers of anything which might be retailed in The Philippines. One can bring in a few bottles of wine for one's own consumption, but loading up dozens of cases of booze would definitely be a no-no unless one has an import licence.

When Asian Tigers were negotiating to get clearance for our shipment, they asked us to provide guarantees that our items were for domestic use only. The 13-A Visa and several other visa classes automatically exempt their holders from import taxes and customs duty.

The following documents must be presented to the final deliverer who will arrange customs inspection and forward local delivery.

Required documentation for customs clearance

1. Original passport with approved/stamped 13-A or 13-G visa
2. Affidavit of legal ownership of the shipment. (The affidavit was sworn at Asian Tigers' office.)
3. Authorization letter (Asian tigers provided a blank for signing and notarization at their office)
4. Original/or NSO copy of the marriage certificate
5. Original/or NSO copy of birth certificates of immigrant and sponsor
6. Alien Registration Certificate (ACR-I card) (The receipt is acceptable since the ACR-I card takes from 5 to 10 days to be processed)
7. Tax account number (TIN)

'NSO' stands for National Statistical Office, the Philippines office where all birth, marriage and death certificates are held.

* * *

Appendix E - immigration rules in The Philippines

There are several ways to get permission to live in The Philippines. One can, for example, retire there whether or not you have a Filipino spouse. The Philippines government is quite welcoming of western retirees, who bring hard currency from their pensions.

Or one can visit as a tourist. One can just turn up at a port of entry and be granted an immediate 21-day visitor's visa. One is required to show one's ticket for exit within the 21 days. Extensions of up to 59 days with a maximum of continuous stay of sixteen months can be obtained from the Bureau of Immigration in Intramuros, Manila. Some travel agents will arrange visa extensions for their clients. One sees them at the Bureau of Immigration offices, clutching stacks of identical visa extension applications.

Foreign spouses of Filipino citizens may also qualify for a one-year visa if they arrive at the immigration desk with the spouse. There is no charge for the one-year visa and it can be awarded at the port of entry at the immigration clerk's discretion. But the foreigner must leave when the year is up.

Foreigners wishing to retire to The Philippines qualify for permanent residence if they are married to a Filipino spouse. They do not have to surrender their foreign citizenship. The usual visa to be applied for is a 13-A. A visitor's visa can be converted to a 13-A by a series of visits (usually three) to the Bureau of Immigration offices and the whole process takes about 2-3 weeks. The 13-A is a probationary visa for one year. One is recommended to apply for permanent residence 2 months before the expiry of the 13-A. After the one-year probationary period, the permanent resident will be given a 13-G visa. Approval is subject to the presentation of bank guarantee certificates to show that you have the necessary funds to support yourself and also to a criminal records check.

Holders of 13-A and 13-G visas may live and work in The Philippines. If they work, then they will also need a tax number of TIN, obtainable from the local tax office in the resident's municipality. Foreign residents - 'non-quota' – do not have full citizenship privileges, though. They cannot buy land or houses attached to lots, although they are allowed to buy single apartments above ground.

The application process for a visa at the Manila office of the Bureau of Immigration is long and frustrating. If you live a long way from the capital, it will be time-consuming and expensive to make the multiple trips. An easy way to shorten the process is to apply for one's 13-A visa at The Philippines embassy in your home country. This can be done quickly and painlessly and will require only one, not three, follow-up visits to the Bureau of Immigration offices.

Filipinos are required to carry ID cards at all times. New holders of the 13-A visa are given a similar card, the Aliens Certificate of Registration Identification, or ACR-I card, which also requires a visit to the BI offices to collect it.

For expatriates not married to Philippines citizens, there exists another option to get permission to retire here. That is by obtaining a Special Resident Retiree Visa or SRRV. For this, you will need to submit proof of your financial viability. The conditions are not onerous – one needs to be at least 50 years old, with a monthly pension of at least $800 and be able to leave on deposit a further $10,000 in a Philippine bank. There is a fee of about $1400. The SRRV is a 'posh' visa and to obtain it, one does not need to mix with the hoi-polloi at the Bureau of Immigration. The entire procedure is a bespoke service offered at the Philippine Retirement Authority (PRA) offices in Citibank Tower in Makati. The Philippines is currently home to over 20,000 holders of the SRRV.

List of documents required for initial application for a 13-A one-year probationary visa

1. Request letter from the petitioner with a statement that all documents submitted were legally obtained from the corresponding government agencies;
2. Duly accomplished and notarized Consolidated General Application Form (BI Form No. RADJR-2012-01); (downloadable)
3. Original copy of NSO issued birth certificate of the Filipino spouse.
4. Original copy of NSO issued Marriage Contract or if the marriage was solemnized abroad, the original copy of the marriage contract authenticated by the Philippine Embassy/Consulate in or nearest the place where the marriage was solemnized, with English translation if written in other foreign language;
5. Photocopy of applicant's passport (bio-page, admission and authorized stay of at least twenty (20) days from date of filing);
6. Original copy of Bureau of Immigration (BI) Clearance Certificate.
7. Joint affidavit of applicant and petitioner attesting to the authenticity and genuineness of all documents submitted in support of the application;
8. Proofs of financial capacity of applicant and/or petitioner during their permanent residence in the Philippines. (Bank guarantee certificates)

Useful websites

The official Bureau of Immigration website is at

http://immigration.gov.ph/

Visa approvals are published here every Monday when the name of the applicant and their sponsor are listed if a visa application has been approved within the previous seven days. From this website, navigate to 'List of BOC acted applications', where visa approvals are listed chronologically.

Very useful, detailed up-to-date information about Philippine immigration procedures can be found at the following excellent site. It includes a lot of useful information about the SRRV.

http://myphilippinelife.com/philippines-retirement-visa-srrv/

Two useful private sites, each with a lot of excellent information are

http://nansphil.com/nansphilen/nans.php
http://real-estate-guide.philsite.net/pra.htm

For UK visa applicants, who might want to apply from Britain, the Philippines Embassy is located at 6-8 Suffolk St London SW1Y 4HG (Tel: 020 7451 1780 or website at http://www.*philembassy-uk.org*). It is easy to find, being just off the north eastern corner of Trafalgar Square, behind the National Gallery

* * *

Appendix F - addresses

Addresses of organizations who provided useful services are

WH Brown, Estate Agents
35/36 Silver Street
Lincoln LN2 1EW
UK
+44 01522 534771   *lincoln@sequencehome.co.uk*

Langley's Solicitors
Olympic House
Doddington Road
Lincoln LN6 3SE
UK
+44 01522 888555   *www.langleys.com*

Monkey Removals Ltd.,
Vulcan Park
George Street
Lincoln LN5 8LG
UK
+44 01522 79 24 34   *www.monkeyremovals.com*

Asian Tigers Lane Moving and Storage
N4 JY & Sons Compound
Veterans Complex
1631 Taguig,
Metro Manila, The Philippines
(632) 838 4835   *www.asiantigers-philippines.com*

Base View Homes
Banaybanay Concepcion,
Lipa City
The Philippines 4217
(043) 756 1830

Victorina Corporation
Banaybanay Concepcion,
Lipa City
The Philippines 4217

* * *

Acknowledgements

A big undertaking like moving one's entire life across continents is not something which is undertaken alone or even as a couple. It requires the assistance of many individuals and organisations. Many of the organisations are, of course, commercial concerns who offer their services in return for payment because that is the way they make their livings. Nevertheless, even those professionals who were incidentally, or closely, involved in our enterprise had the option of being either helpfully friendly or coldly impersonal. Either manner would not have compromised the high level of competence we encountered. Maybe it is because both my wife, Loydz, and I tend towards seeing the best in human nature that the general level of professionalism we encountered throughout our project was invariably accompanied by warmth and friendliness. To all those who helped us, whether paid or unpaid, we offer our deepest thanks and warmest best wishes.

The commercial outfits we came into contact with included the HSBC Bank in Lincoln High Street, where Donna Coy was extremely helpful in changing our status from mere domestic account holders to the sort of people who move money from one country to another, just like those clever people in the City of London.

WHBrown, the estate agents who sold our English house, were a solid reproach to the usual cynical view of that much-maligned profession. They were competent, straight-dealing and efficient. Sarah, their front desk face, took an interest in our sale and I am delighted to be able to congratulate her for her unfailing friendliness and helpfulness.

Langleys of Lincoln, our British lawyers, proved themselves to be eminently capable. They handled our little transaction as if it were much bigger and more important than it really was, as true professionals invariably do. Thanks to Sarah Elderkin and Jemma Parker of Langleys for their unfailing friendliness and efficiency.

Then there were the packers, Monkey Removals of Lincoln and their boss, Tim, who provided a very thorough comprehensive door-to-door service from packing up even the kitchen minutiae of our house in England and delivering it eight thousand miles later to have it capably and thoroughly unpacked by the very competent Asian Tigers of Taguig, Manila, under the expert management of Ms Sol Sia. It was as if we just moved the entire house, lock, stock and barrel, from one country and set it down unchanged in another, so simple did both companies make the process.

In The Philippines, we must pay tribute to our builder, Vic Maralit, who did his building on time and within budget with a jovial and expansive personality. His workmen, especially Buddy, the foreman, just known to all as 'Foreman' and Randy the electrician, were unstinting helpfulness itself. We must also mention the staff at Base View Homes who have quickly become our friends. Myla, a landscape artist *par excellence*, did a wonderful job of turning our building site into something which, under the warm Philippine sun and Loydz' constant attention, will surely mature into a truly beautiful garden.

Many of Loydz' large extended family have shown us help, support and kindness including Jay and Apple, my stepson and stepdaughter and their families, Cousin Leony and her husband Rufino, Loydz' sister, Ith and her brother Manny. We also thank Cousin Winnie and her husband Louis, whose car we bought at a generous price.

We owe a deep debt of gratitude to Cousin Oswald and wife Amy whose condominium near Manila airport was our first temporary home in The Philippines while the finishing touches were being put to the new house.

Most of all, we must thank Cousin Cosette, to whom this book is dedicated and who always gave so generously of her time taking us around our new home town. She was always available to drive us to whatever office we needed to go to in Lipa, where, as a long-term Lipeña, she knows everybody and knows where everything is to be found. Her local knowledge, and her inexhaustible energy were invaluable. We are also certainly deeply grateful to Cosette's husband, Bobi, who also gave his help open-handedly, particularly when it came to negotiating with the municipal authorities.

I have not included my dear wife Loydz in the list of those whom we are thanking here. That is because it was entirely a joint venture. She proved herself to be a very competent project manager and organised the building in Lipa while I was involved in the selling up in Lincoln. It is an old cliché to say that we are a team but on this occasion, the parallel execution of the two halves of the project was in almost perfect symmetry.

ISBN 978-971-95780-0-0

www.ingramcontent.com/pod-product-compliance
Lightning Source LLC
Chambersburg PA
CBHW071513040426
42444CB00008B/1619